BEYOND
Intellect

JOURNEY

INTO THE

WISDOM

OF YOUR

INTUITIVE

MIND

Open,
Accept,
and Allow!

Warmly,
Susan

Susan McNeal Velasquez

Beyond Intellect
Journey Into the Wisdom of Your Intuitive Mind
Susan McNeal Velasquez

Copyright © 2007
Row Your Boat Press. All rights reserved.
Published by Row Your Boat Press, Laguna Beach, Ca.

ISBN: 978-0-9796410-0-8
Publishing Strategist: Jan B. King, www.janbking.com
Editor: Christine Frank, www.christinefrank.com
Proofreader: Laura Beggins, labeggins@sbc.comglobal.net
Index: Christine Frank, www.christinefrank.com
Cover and Interior Design: Toolbox Creative. www/toolboxcreative.com

Library of Congress Cataloguing-in-Publications Data
Library of Congress Control Number: 2007933185
Susan McNeal Velasquez
Beyond Intellect
Journey Into the Wisdom of Your Intuitive Mind
ISBN: 978-0-9796410-0-8
2007

Beyond Intellect :: Contents

~~~ FOREWORD

Imagine this: I am sitting in a little Laguna Beach café, giving myself a moment to re-group before taking on the next round of commitments I have for the day. I glance up to see a notice posted on the wall. "Unleash the Power of Your Intuition." My eyes follow down to the message that says: "Are you ready to take life to the next level?"

The next level? Life is seeming like a Rubik's cube of tangled emotions. At times, you make progress. You line up two rows only to find the others jumbled up, time and time again. You are clear, open, and organized in some areas, while other areas of you are locked into the wrong sequence. At times, it feels like a labyrinth with no exit. Lots of action, lots of forward movement, only to arrive at what often seem like dead ends. You know life is an adventure, but do you have to climb Mt. Everest everyday?

With some excitement, some trepidation, you grab the brochure and dial the number. That day begins the voyage inward - a voyage *beyond intellect*. A voyage that unleashes your intuition. A day that miraculously transforms your life forever. That day was my day.

This day is your day. You've reached for this book and you're ready. Ready to move from scared to the sacred. From perfect to real. From surviving to thriving.

You're ready to learn to ride the ebbs and flows of life without drowning in an Olympic-size pool of your emotional soup. You'll learn to navigate and balance the positive and negative, the water and fire, the ups and downs, the male and female. You'll learn life mastery.

Begin this wonderful love affair with life, where miracles come in all shapes and sizes. Go beyond your intellect and discover a new, likable you. Re-ignite your passions and unlock your unique secret coding. Unravel the internal wiring that has kept you hostage to your inner critic. Allow your intellect to work harmoniously with your intuition and you will see the creation of a positive realignment creating positive outcomes.

Beyond Intellect: Journey Into the Wisdom of Your Intuitive Mind offers you a fresh approach and a new perspective. You will cherish this book. It will become a mainstay in your self-improvement journey.

Coralee Newman
Founder & CEO
Government Solutions, Inc.
Newport Beach, Ca

～ PREFACE

For the past fourteen years, I have been writing and producing weekly seminars that focus on the topic of intuition. I have also been writing a weekly newspaper column on the same topic for twelve years.

The information in this book is the convergence of insights amassed from both sources, as well as from my thirty-four years of experience presenting personal development seminars.

Beyond Intellect: Journey Into The Wisdom of Your Intuitive Mind is the love-child born from the exquisite privilege and pleasure of authoring my own life by doing what I love, in ways that make sense to me.

Throughout my career, I have had many opportunities to be involved as a catalyst for change through the presentation of personal development seminars to both large and small audiences across the United States.

The major benefit of my years in this field is that I have witnessed the miraculous healing power of hearing the truth told simply and profoundly. When our mind is open and our heart swells with understanding and compassion, it is because we have found our intuitive voice.

I am no longer interested in being what is known as "a sage on the stage." Instead, I wholeheartedly embrace the opportunity to be "a guide on the side."

It is my hope that the information contained in this book will give you clear guidance, direction, and useful insights into the choices that you can immediately put into practice to create a full, rich connection to the pulses of your life's energies.

I look forward to traveling right next to you on this journey within.

Use This Book in a New Way

If you are currently facing a situation that has you doubting yourself and you are confused about what is the right action to take –

Do this:

> Hold the book between your two hands. Ask this question: What specifically do I need to know at this time? Take a few gentle breaths, pause, and allow the book to open wherever it wants. Read what is provided.

If you have time to do some soul-searching and feel excited about savoring the experience of discovering new insights –

Do this:

> Bring writing material and give yourself permission to elaborate on the thoughts and feelings that are generated by your reading. Delve into the segments that talk to you and take time to answer some of the questions that intrigue you.

If you are too busy to have any meaningful alone time –

Do this:

> Put the book by your bed. Read a few pages before you go to sleep. Give yourself credit for committing the time to intentionally focus inward for a few moments and allow your subconscious to do the rest.

Get ready to connect your intellect with the wisdom of your intuitive mind to spark one of the most powerful journeys you can take: the journey within.

Susan McNeal Velasquez, Laguna Beach, California

INTRODUCTION

Imagine that this book is like a kaleidoscope. There are basic stones in the form of concepts, statements, and imaginings that make up each design. Red, orange, yellow, green, blue, purple, lavender, and white stones continually show up to form an endless array of configurations.

Each design is slightly or significantly different from the last. The variations are endless in the land beyond intellect, where all aspects of ourselves can commune to form new and varied opportunities to spark specific and timely insights.

Normally our intellect is the designated driver. *Beyond Intellect: Journey Into the Wisdom of Your Intuitive Mind* is designed to allow your intellect to take the co-pilot position so that it can finally rest from problem-solving and daydream for a bit.

A transformational leap in self-knowledge and mastery is well within your reach when you encourage your intellect to relax so that your imaginative mind can be rekindled, rejuvenated, and renewed.

This book is written for the reader who has amassed enough answers and is secure enough within to ask himself or herself the deeper questions that go beyond self-centered or other-centered to the place where soul-centered resides.

When our lives are moving at breakneck speeds and our eyes are rigidly locked on future external goals, we miss the subtleties and nuances of life. We cannot connect with our inner guidance or resources because we have opted for life in the fast lane.

We fast-forward through the labyrinth of our minds and hearts and then we complain when we are stuck with lives that "aren't too pretty but we make great time."

When we shift our focus from seeing our lives as a never-ending problem to be solved and open to our unique life as a reality to be fully experienced, we can begin to accept and flow with the shifts and changes that allow increased personal expansion of our understanding, knowledge, and peace of mind.

Perhaps it is high time to make new choices that begin to connect us with the exquisite sensitivity within our deepest being.

Our inner wisdom can express and acknowledge our passionate longings and our emotion-laden heart hurts and can disclose crippling criticisms; in so doing, we are forever touched and transformed by the beauty and bravery of what it means to be authentically human.

It takes a strong and flexible intellect to be willing to hold the paradox of actively assessing who we are today while envisioning our future by musing, visualizing, and courting our highest and best vision of who we will become.

The benefit of going beyond what we already know, by exercising the mental muscle of visualization and imagination, is that we can transform our lives away from endless striving for elusive perfection and move towards increased authenticity and the experience of thriving.

As a result, we effortlessly shift towards life choices that enhance our sense of our basic goodness and the basic goodness of our lives.

This book is designed to assist you to access your own feelings, thoughts, wishes, hopes, dreams, and visions for your future.

We will move beyond the usual problem-solving stance that categorizes and locks our thoughts and feelings into compartments labeled good/bad and right/wrong. We will open and explore the doors marked soften, open, deepen, and strengthen to discover what will work to transform our lives from striving to thriving.

In order to ensure that our experience together is timely rather than time-bound, energizing rather than overwhelming, and inspiring rather than threatening, I want to establish specific guidelines so that we can easily and effortlessly navigate through the information presented without overloading your intellect or your emotions.

I am going to ask you to consider the following ten questions. If you can, to the best of your present ability, answer yes to each question, you will be ready to glean the most benefit from the information you will be receiving.

1. *Are you willing to consider that there is a purpose for your life that is bigger than your current moment-to-moment thoughts and feelings, and that this is the next step for you?*

2. *Are you willing to slow down enough to read each segment so that you can decide whether it is necessary information for you to open to, take in, and connect to your life?*

3. *Are you willing to skip segments that don't talk specifically to you without making yourself or the material wrong?*

4. *Are you willing to open the doors of your intellect to the experience of "not knowing" to allow new information to expand your thinking or to allow old information to reconfigure into new and useful insights that you can use now?*

5. *Are you willing to stop reading whenever you start to feel overloaded, overwhelmed, or satisfied and full, even if you have read only a few pages?*

6. *Are you willing to refrain from using this information to criticize or condemn yourself or others and instead give yourself permission to re-read a segment until you can fully absorb the information and use it to enhance your understanding of situations you are currently facing?*

7. *Are you willing to stay focused on your own process of growth and intentionally bypass the temptation to try to counsel, teach, or fix anyone else?*

8. *Are you willing to test and experiment with the information rather than immediately rejecting it or immediately believing it, so that you can use your personal experience to determine what is true and useful to you?*

9. *Are you willing to be gentle with yourself and patient with your new insights by taking all the time you need to savor this journey?*

10. *Are you willing to allow yourself to welcome orphaned feelings; discarded hopes and dreams; buried and abandoned desires; and new, exciting and unanticipated creative ideas to begin to show themselves to you?*

With your *yes* answers in place, we are ready to begin our journey. Remember to simply give yourself permission to be open and receptive to the information that seems to talk specifically to you. Then listen, gently and patiently, for your intuitive guidance, always through the basic method of cherishing, honoring, and respecting yourself and others.

CHAPTER 1   GOING BEYOND INTELLECT TO DISCOVER YOUR LIFE PATH

You have a life path that is uniquely your own. At first glance, this path may look more like a high-wire act, with you being a novice tightrope walker without a net.

By adding a leap of faith, a change in mental visualization, and the willingness to court a stronger sense of self-trust, a wide path will appear that you can firmly place your feet upon. Your path will become more real to you, as we continue on our journey together.

Following your life path is a full-participation sport.

The first challenge is to let go of the intellectual notion of "the perfect life," planned to deliver to you, free of charge, all the benefits that life has to offer with none of the prices.

Surrendering the prepackaged perfect plan allows you to begin your journey on the road to real.

The road to real shows up one step at a time. Following it requires as much patience and courage as you can muster up. It also asks you to willingly befriend "not knowing" until your marching orders arrive by special delivery from the Universe, addressed to you personally.

Let's begin by opening your mind and softening your heart in anticipation of receiving new guidance and directions.

The Road to Real

Imagine with me for a moment that you are the owner of a magnificent painting. A Monet, Picasso, or Rembrandt. It is priceless, a one-of-a-kind.

What would you do? Hang it in your living room? Tell everyone who comes to visit all about it? Be delighted by your good fortune? Worry that it will be stolen or damaged? Decide it is too much trouble and worry, so you sell it? Hide it away in a vault so nothing can happen to it? Pause here for a moment to run these images through your mind.

Owning something of value brings responsibilities with it and choices to be made.

Perhaps that is why so many of us hide our brilliance. Our majesty. Our uniqueness. We are afraid. Afraid we will be ripped off. Damaged. Used up.

We take our original masterpiece, our authentic selves, and make a duplicate. It looks good and is a reasonable facsimile. We think we are saving our genuineness for the really important times. We lock our authenticity away in a safety vault where no one can get to it.

We rationalize this behavior by saying it makes sense. Why waste genuine feelings, openness, and honesty on mundane situations? Why put ourselves in jeopardy? Most people can't tell the difference between real and pretense anyway. It is much safer this way and besides, we *do* own the original. We are not lying about having a masterpiece. We are just being prudent.

Here is the problem. **There is a vast difference between an original and a duplicate. It has to do with energy. Vibrancy. Vitality.**

When we make a commitment to living our lives authentically, life heats up. When we decide to focus on real instead of perfect, we stop pretending. We start to thaw out. Un-numb. Defrost. Resurrect from the dead. We begin to feel. We become aware of our hidden emotions, both negative and positive.

We begin to come in contact with our unresolved fear, jealousy, hatred, revenge, greed, anger, and resentment. We awaken our sleeping creativity, faith, love, enthusiasm, and hope.

This calls for bravery on our part. A special kind of bravery that is defined as the courage to live in the world without the self-deception of pretending to be better than or less than anyone else.

It requires the courage to approach life with kindness and caring for ourselves and others.

When we develop this kind of bravery, we become connected with the elemental qualities of existence. We begin to bring out the brilliant, authentic qualities of our being.

We begin to live our lives as the priceless masterpieces we are.

The road to perfect and the road to real will intertwine until the day comes when we reach a fork in the road that requires a choice.

If we choose to continue to lust after elusive perfection, our focus will remain external. Our center of being is surrendered to the god of doing. Our core grounding seats itself in scared instead of sacred.

When we begin to view our life force, our energy, as sacred, we step up to accept the responsibility of being a co-creator with a greater power than ours.

The sacred and the mundane marry and learn to walk side by side on the road to real, as we raise our energy to create a wind of sacred delight, power, and vitality in our lives.

A Path With Heart

The intellect is associated with knowledge, intelligence, information gathering, and the production of tangible outcomes.

The imagery associated with the heart usually links it to love, passion, feelings, emotions, and the softer side of life's experiences.

In our fast-moving, make-it-happen society, matters of the heart are often relegated to a backseat position. As a result, the more production-oriented we become, the more we are in danger of signing up and committing to a life without heart.

What do I mean? Because of the amount of information we are subjected to daily, one of the skills necessary for survival is a high level of selective perception. In other words, we only see what we deem important enough to see.

What we value determines what gets our attention.

Our core values drive our decisions. Even if we are unaware of what our values are, we will consistently make our choices based on that unexplored value system.

When our core values are unacknowledged and ignored, the stage is set for the repeated creation of drama and upsets that leave us frustrated, confused, and unhappy with our lives.

The Midas Touch in Reverse

When your life isn't working the way you want it to, it is helpful to pinpoint exactly how you are being destructive and then set about taking full responsibility for the part of the 'train wreck' that is yours.

First you must get over the general inclination we all have for justifying our actions, invalidating others, and collecting significant clues that add up to an airtight case that pronounces us right and somebody or something else wrong. Once you stop trying to prove how right you are, you can recover your power to choose.

The significant question is: What are you choosing? Where do you habitually put your attention? Nobody wants to be wrong. In our heart of hearts, we are all doing the very best we can. Though it may not look like it, everyone is coping, making it, and standing up to the challenges with everything they currently have available.

As a matter of fact, one of the more popular ways that we avoid being wrong is by putting too much time, attention, and effort into solving 'the problem.'

There is a saying that we never get enough of what we really don't want. The double negatives in this sentence are brain-stoppers that can be useful to help us derail our obsessive, frantic, overachieving minds for a moment.

What does "We never get enough of what we really don't want" mean? When we are desperately lusting after a solution to a perceived problem, we use our power to create in reverse. For example, let's use 'looking for love' as the problem.

You decide it is time to create the relationship of your dreams. You are feeling more secure about yourself and you feel you are ready to share your life with another. Your intention is to find or attract love into your life in the form of an intimate partner with whom you are compatible. You have set your intention. The Universe is listening. The manifestation machinery has just been turned on. Next comes forward movement towards the creation of the desired result. Or does it?

Let's go back and look closely at the stated intention. You want to find or attract love into your life. Which is it? Find equals seeking, as in searching to discover something of unexpected value. Attract means to draw toward, to cause to approach.

"I don't care. I just want it to happen!" you say impatiently. The Universe yawns and responds back: "If you don't care, I don't care" and continues to spin on.

If you are aggressively demanding your perfect match, look around. He or she is showing up daily. Every time anyone speaks or acts aggressively and demandingly to get their needs met, they will be a match for you.

Your range of experiential matches will be on the aggressive-submissive spectrum. It will be possible for you to find only overly aggressive people who vibrate at the same frequency as you or extremely passive, submissive people who will have enough empty, stagnant space around them to house your over-aggressive, frantic energy.

This is not what you had in mind? This is a perfect example of how you never get enough of what you really don't want. Your intention is unclear and your energetic stance is impatient, demanding, and counterproductive to creating partnerships.

Most of us have never been taught how important clear intent is to the process of creating what we want.

Intention is the point of conception. It is the DNA of our desires. It is the beginning and the end. It is the point of power.

Spending quality time to get crystal clear on exactly what you want will ensure the manifestation of your desired result. One hundred percent guaranteed.

There are two distinct ways to evaluate what is happening in our lives. We can either turn our attention to acknowledging all of our results, both positive and negative, and then put into action new choices that will work more effectively, or we can use our attention to document all of the reasons why we don't have the results we want.

Understanding is what we get when we want to be right by having the right answers. **Being the 'answer person' is impressive in academia but is one of the most disastrous stumbling blocks to creating a magnificent life.**

Asking a 'why' question is a dead-end street. Every why question needs a 'because' answer. Why did you do that? Why didn't you do this? Well, because. Then come the justifications, explanations, and endless analyzing; a huge waste of time and energy. Instead, activate your dream machine.

Open the door to your creative energy by training yourself to ask 'what' questions instead of 'why.'

What does your heart desire? What is true for you? What do you need to enliven in your life? What is hurting or harming you? What are you avoiding? What do you want? What are you waiting for? What can you do now? What will you do? What are you really about? The questions that will rev up your engine are endless.

We don't need to answer all of these questions today. We simply need to open to the willingness to entertain questions that yield answers beyond good and bad, right and wrong.

Decide to take your focus off making yourself right or wrong, good or bad, and turn your full light of intention and attention on what will work for you and what doesn't work. Do what works. Say *yes* to what works. Say *no* to what doesn't work. Stand in the present moment. Set a clear intention. Ask for intuitive guidance and direction and listen for your next step. Stay focused on the horizon of your anticipated results. Start now.

Making Changes Now

Past. Present. Future. When we glimpse our lives through these different points of view, we get a superb opportunity to glean information that can positively empower us in the present and inform our decisions.

Imagine yourself waking up tomorrow with a solid sense of who you are, without any of the residual pain from past decisions or experiences that didn't turn out the way you'd hoped.

You are fully connected to your essence energy and are thoroughly confident and capable of successfully managing your life with clarity and positive enthusiasm.

You are solidly planted in the present; able to say yes when you mean yes and no when you mean no, without hesitation or confusion. If it were possible to rewind the tape of your life and revisit *every* choice from your past when you said yes to situations and you really meant no, you would be able to discover and uncover your choice points that were made for the purpose of managing your image in the world.

You would find how many times you said yes to get another's approval, to please other people, to being controlled or manipulated, and to giving up your commitment to your own needs, values, thoughts, and feelings in favor of trying to fit in or look good.

If we could revisit the past and look for every time you said no to opportunities and situations when you really wanted to say yes, we would discover how you turned down the volume, dimmed the lights, and closed the door to your heart's desires.

We would uncover how you allowed your enthusiasm and spontaneous, joyful anticipation of future hopefulness and happiness to be reduced to a trickle.

If it were possible to get a detailed readout of each time you said yes when you really meant no and no when you really meant yes, we would have an extremely accurate road map of how you became who you are today.

> *Self-mastery comes from the ability to stand firmly in the present, aware of the fact that the point of our personal power to choose is always rooted in the present.*

When we commit to living in the present as though we are were equipped with everything we need to know, our past can then visit us, bringing gifts of insight into where we made choices out of fear and ignorance and the prices and benefits that came to us as a result.

It takes courage to hone the skill of cutting through the debris of our past like a fine surgeon who doesn't cut without also being able to suture a wound.

The past longs to gift us with usable insights that, when melded into our present, will give us the wisdom to make broader, more conscious, and discerning choices today.

There is alchemy at work when our past, our present, and our future convene in the present moment.

Does this seem like an impossible task? Does the thought of welcoming your past home feel impossible or overwhelming to you? Are you holding yourself hostage to what you think might be unredeemable mistakes?

Are you living out a prison sentence by shuffling through the present, unwilling or unable to envision or anticipate a future that is alive with enthusiasm and renewed innocence?

I am going to let you in on an important secret. You can take a shortcut to be freed from the debilitating aspects of a too-serious approach to being personally responsible for all the good and bad aspects of your life.

Here it is: Recall one clear incident from your near present that is worthy of this statement: "I wouldn't have missed this for the world." It may be an experience of a person, a place, a situation, a job, a vacation, a one-time interaction, or simply a kiss from Grace that touched your body, mind, heart, and soul simultaneously. Pause here for a moment and savor the memory. Let the remembered feelings trickle into your heart and re-activate a sense of inner satisfaction.

Make the choice to embrace, acknowledge, and fully own just one of those moments. As a result of this one seemingly simple decision, you can give yourself permission to show up, in this present moment, fully formed and ready to create anew.

How can that be? Look closely and you will see the logic: This perfect moment could not exist and would not have happened without every previous moment that came before it, bad or good, right or wrong.

Our past is. Our present is. Our future is seeded in this present moment.

The point of power is in the present. Gather up all the delight in life you can. Breathe it in and courageously step into your future right now.

An Invitation to Life

Remember when you were a child who couldn't wait to grow up so you could pick your own clothes, eat what you chose, stay out as late as you like, and all the rest?

Some of us came into the world ready and willing to jump into the game. Ready-fire-aim children require vigilant parents holding on to the back of their shirttails so that they don't jump off of every cliff they are faced with, just for the thrill of it.

Other children see dragons and demons around every corner and are more content to watch the show than venture out and put themselves in the fray. Most of us made it through our childhood with a mixture of both extremes.

Today we are looking for a lost part of you that is still holding back from fully participating in your life. This part is hidden in the dark and is waiting for someone to give it permission to step out into the light of today.

Imagine that you are spiraling back into your childhood to recapture that feeling of true excitement about life. Stay with each remembering as you bring that long-ago exuberance into the present.

- ⁓ Remember when you couldn't wait to get up in the morning and were never ready to go to bed at night.

- ⁓ Remember getting new sneakers and knowing that you really could run faster.

- ⁓ Remember the smell of freshly mowed grass and spinning around and around until the ground came up to meet you.

- Remember going barefoot in the summer and feeling the heat from the sidewalk on your feet.

- Remember quickly climbing a tree to the highest branches and then being frozen with fear on the slow, treacherous way down.

- Remember fast, fierce fights with friends.

- Remember shrieking and yelling and jumping and running.

- Remember laughing while making up crazy games and elaborate plans with your best friend of the moment.

- Remember *star light, star bright, first star I see tonight* and making wishes you knew would come true.

Now bring your mind back to the present, the you of today. Bring that remembered exuberance along with you as you begin to muse on questions that can open new doors of discovery.

1. *What is missing from your life at this time? Pause here for a moment until missed feelings or experiences surface.*

2. *What would you love to do that would be out of the ordinary for you but would lighten and brighten your life?*

3. *What would you need to let go of in order to allow yourself to have new experiences of the delightful kind? Where are you presently stifling your self-expression?*

Can you entertain giving yourself permission to honestly answer those questions? If not, it may be that your inner critic is excessively vigilant and firmly established as your own internal, critical parent. Discipline gone haywire.

The reasons for squelching things that interest and attract us are many. "It's not practical. No time. No money. Too frivolous. I'd feel too uncomfortable, silly, and irresponsible. I already have too much to do."

The real issue is that most of us have forgotten how to be fun, do fun things, or have fun. We are boring, bored, numbed out, and on automatic pilot, trudging through our endless lists of roles and responsibilities.

We are locked into being adults. High rollers. Big-impact people who are interested only in the important things. We're about big changes.

We are waiting for just the right time. Then we will make all the right moves and when that time comes, watch out world!

Our inner longing says: "When can we?" and we reply: "Soon, but not just yet."

This is where a shift in perception must be made. Profound shifts come in small and seemingly inconsequential ways. Simple little experiences fully embraced feed the exuberant child within.

Once again, remember.

⌒ Teenage years. The thrill of simply holding hands. Tender kisses. Walks on the beach. Slow dancing. Pause here for a moment.

⌒ The electricity of attraction. Being flooded with emotions. The experience of really listening and being listened to while trying to, first time, talk about new and unexplored feelings.

⌒ Remember the exquisite, tumultuous, heart-stopping, hopeful, rejuvenating experience of first love? Recall this memory as fully as you can.

⌒ And remember the pain when the rocket of heightened sensing and experience fueled by impossible expectations came crashing down and landed in a rubble of dreams turned to ashes?

Why would I ask you to recall the pain? Here is why. **The key to our disowned passion for life is hidden in the ashes of our worst disasters.**

When we can truly face head-on the heart-hurts of our lives, we have a chance to grab the elusive brass ring. When we can admit that we are vulnerable to exquisite heartache, when we can directly face and own that we are vulnerable and have been hurt, a miraculous thing happens.

We start to realize, slowly at first and then with more momentum, that we are still here. We are still whole. We are not damaged, used up, broken and thrown away, less than, or unable.

When we acknowledge that we are whole, we can begin to own our wisdom. Our intuition can finally become a fully participating partner in the creation of the next phase of our lives.

> *The task before us is simply to become an awake, aware person with new choices to make.*

Life invites us, each and every moment, to participate and it is our pleasure and privilege to accept or decline.

This may be the simplest truth. We each have the right to say yes or no to life. The truly miraculous gift is that life continues to ask, moment by full, rich, potent moment.

> *We cannot be fully alive until we allow our intuitive selves to take us home, back to that place where we can uncover and discover what our soul longs for.*

Chapter 2 DEFINING WHAT YOU LONG FOR

Intention versus Attention

Imagine if the ocean could decide that high tide is the only accept-able form it can take and therefore will not acknowledge low tide as a part of the ebb and flow of its natural life. Like clockwork, each and every time low tide presented itself, the justifications and posturing the ocean would have to do to maintain its high-tide image would be staggering, all-consuming, counter-productive, and ridiculous to even contemplate.

Being special, being somebody, is the unspoken mandate that crowds our airwaves and is contaminating our capacity for compas-sion, camaraderie, and connection with ourselves and others. If we are devoid of any deeper motivation than seeking out and getting attention, then our soul's intellectual eye and therefore, our creative energies, will be invested in a self-centeredness that becomes a form of idol worship.

When we create an idealized version of ourselves that can't possibly be reached or maintained, we freeze our natural ebb and flow of creative energy into a stagnant container that holds no room for discovery, curi-osity, passion, or vitality.

Rather than unconsciously pursuing the path of striving to be the *center of special attention, perhaps it is time to set the intention to* discover and uncover our ability to create a meaning–filled life that fosters opportunities to make our unique contributions.

Perhaps it is time to allow ourselves more room to partner with, learn about, and respect the ebb and flow of our natural rhythm which will open us to increased tranquility and peace of mind.

A Treasure Hunt

When we turn our mind's eye inward, insight can come to visit. Let's turn away from the external bombardment for a moment and listen. Listen for that still, small voice within that beckons us to follow a simpler, kinder, more compassionate path that unfolds gently, one step at a time.

We will begin our journey beyond intellect by asking your intuitive wisdom to lead you to a symbol that represents an answer to the following question: **What aspect of yourself do you want to consciously open up to and embrace in order to further your soul growth?** You see, the intuition speaks through symbols. We are now asking your intuition to guide you towards your next step.

Look for an object. A picture. An expression of nature. Your symbol may be something in your home that you already treasure or, as you muse about what qualities you want to actualize, you may see something in your environment that you can use as a visual reminder of your essence goal.

Do not expect a tidy, easy answer. Muse, dream, wonder, imagine. Is there a small seed of potential in need of cultivation that is calling to you? That is your next step?

At this point, there may be a part of you that wants to stop reading. "What does she mean, find a symbol or object?" Hocus, pocus, says our intellect.

But this is not mystical, magical thinking. Our intuitive mind works through pictures, not words. We draw descriptive words provided through our intellect after our intuition feeds us pictures. Don't take my word for it. Close your eyes and see if you can envision a fuller and richer life for yourself. What do you see? Even if the picture is not clear, you can feed the vision by clarifying what qualities you want to actualize within yourself to create the climate for a more satisfying life. Take some time here. Savor these creative pictures.

What qualities do you want to open up to and embrace to enrich your life experiences? Are you longing to be more creative, compassionate, self-accepting, personally powerful, safe, exuberant, at peace, and free to express yourself fully?

Continue to visualize that new life. Allow your mind to play out scenarios that make you smile and feel warm and at home. Allow your mind to play out scenarios that entice you to envision a fuller and richer life. What aspects of yourself do you need to open to and embrace so that you can attract this new reality? Listen closely and hear your inner yearnings.

Allow yourself to enjoy these moments. Activate your heart's intelligence and your intellect's passion to envision your life as fulfilling and satisfying as you can imagine.

Try to actively identify what stimulates your mind and sparks your innate creativity. Find a concrete symbol as an out-picturing of the experiences and qualities you most want to open up to, embrace, and actualize in your life.

Use the information you just collected to take the next step: to begin the process of deepening your ability to accept and trust your inner guidance.

Once you take this first step of commiting to finding one unique symbol, we can activate the skill of accessing your intuitive wisdom through the use of an I Am statement.

We will use this symbol to spark your intellect's participation in the creation of your first I Am statement.

⌒ *A Message From Your Guide:*

Note: I am aware that in order for you to carry out this assignment, you will be required to stop reading and actually take whatever time is necessary to find your symbol. It is inconvenient, disrupts the flow, and also asks you to switch gears from passive, receptive energy to taking action to produce a specific outcome.

The good news is that if you are willing to push through any resistance and find a symbol, I promise it will be worth the effort.

You see, using a symbol as the catalyst to engage your intuition is the most effective way I have discovered to start the process of creating a partnership between your intuition and your intellect.

Your intuition will guide you to select the most timely symbol to answer the question: "What aspect of yourself do you want to consciously open up to and embrace to further your soul growth?"

Choosing a symbol puts your intuition in the driver's seat. Allowing your intellect to choose the words that make up your I Am statement puts your intellect and your emotions in the co-pilot position.

Once you have chosen your symbol, you can continue on with the next segment to create your first I Am statement.

I Am...

An I Am statement is a series of words chosen by you that expresses your desire to expand into and own the qualities you are naming in the statement. It is formulated in the present tense and starts with the words I Am.

This statement is fashioned from your own wisdom about yourself and is formulated in words specifically chosen by you. This is a statement that will serve as a continuous reminder of your future visualized self and the expanded life that will unfold for you as a result. It serves as a link between what you saw as possible in your mind's eye (the first statement in each pair below) with ownership of these qualities right now (the second statement in italics).

Some examples:

- I see myself painting in my studio and then selling my artwork.

- *I am creative and innovative.*

- I see myself with my teenage children on a wonderful vacation to Hawaii, having some time to get to know each other before they go off to college.

- *I am accepting of myself and others.*

- I bought a new house in a neighborhood I love close to the ocean and am very happy living there.

- *I am safe and secure.*

- I am excited about thinking of the possibilities of a new relationship.

- *I am loved and loving.*

- I am saying no to the intrusions of my extended family and putting myself and my needs ahead of saying yes just to appease people.

- *I am owning my own power.*

- I'm going to take my restlessness to write and spend time on it, perhaps converting it to a career one day.

- *I am respecting and listening to my inner guidance.*

Writing your statement in the present tense, as if it were already true, is crucial. Stating your inner vision in the present tense allows you to attract those circumstances to you that will help turn this statement into reality. All you will need is a bit of self-trust and patience.

You can use this statement as your internal guidance system. It will assist you in knowing what experiences to say yes to: the experiences that will allow you to further this vision. It will give your emotions and intellect a way to work together for a common purpose.

By committing to an I Am statement that is borne out of your desire to consciously embrace and own more of your true essence, you actively begin the process of intentional living. By discovering, uncovering, and committing your spirit, mind, and heart to one intentional statement stated in the present tense, you allow your every action to be in alignment with those beliefs and the Universe begins to act accordingly, bringing those things to you.

Letting Go

Your next assignment is to find another picture or object, this time one that represents an aspect of yourself that you want to consciously let go of.

As an example, a participant at one of my seminars brought in a small piece of rope to the session on letting go. She tied the rope into a miniature noose, which she called the Noose of Negativity.

This became her touchstone and her inner direction to say no to negative thoughts and feelings in her day-to-day life. Once again, it is very important to take whatever time is needed to find a specific symbol that represents your letting go.

Create another statement, again in the present tense, of what you want to let go of. Something that you struggle with now that is blocking and restricting you from fully expressing your best self.

The same participant I mentioned created this Letting Go statement:

I am letting go of the noose of negativity.

If you are having trouble with these statements, take a look in the Appendix of this book for some more examples that might help to spark your own creativity.

By establishing an I Am statement and a Letting Go statement, you are beginning your personal process of intentional living. These two statements, created by your inner, intuitive knowledge about yourself, will be used to guide you and inform you on what experiences to say yes to and what to say no to.

Why is this so important? You have many skills, talents, and abilities that you have already developed. There are many paths that are open to you and therefore many choices available. If you have no awareness of what serves your highest purpose, you may wander aimlessly through life with no direction or you may scatter your energies by taking on too many directions at one time.

If you decide to live your life taking direction from others or following someone else's rules and regulations, you can easily do that. You simply get a list of the rules to follow and do what you are told.

But what if you want to be the author of your own life? What if you long to discover, uncover, and follow your unique, one-of-a-kind timing, rhythm, and tempo as you move through the rest of your life? If this is what you desire, it is crucial that you understand the importance of having a specific method that will allow you to set your own intentions in place.

We use the I Am and Letting Go statements as directional reins. Remember, the statements come directly from the symbols, which are chosen by you. Out of the myriad objects in the world, you intentionally chose two. Not ten or twenty, just two. Completing these two assignments represents your first step in following your own intuitive wisdom.

Once you've established your I Am and I Am Letting Go statements, there is an interesting phenomenon that immediately takes place. Since we are establishing our statements in the present tense we are actually claiming ownership of these statements immediately.

Here. Now. In this present moment. Not tomorrow or the next day or some day in the future. We are stating and taking ownership immediately.

Your I Am and I Am Letting Go statements are well-thought-out expressions of your essence self. They are not future goals.

Goal-setting is an external process of progressively moving towards the manifestation of external results. Traditional goal setting uses 'make it happen' energy.

Your I Am and I Am Letting Go statements are an expression of the experience you desire from what you are longing for. This is a very important distinction.

When you courageously declare that you are taking possession of these qualities immediately, you activate your ability to attract all manner of opportunities to express these qualities.

The I Am Principle entices allowing, receptive, intuitive energy to enter into your life.

Choosing and committing to one clear I Am and one Letting Go allows your intellect and intuition to enter into a full partnership that will yield potent guidance and direction that will come to you, one step and one experience at a time.

Congratulations on taking this important step. Giving yourself permission to act beyond your intellect to establish these two statements will set your feet firmly on your unique inner path, fashioned by your willingness to listen to your deeper intuitive knowledge about what is the right action for you at this particular time in your life.

Write your I Am statement and Letting Go statement here:

⌒ **I am** _____

⌒ **I am letting go of** _____

Taming Your Inner Critic

One of the major benefits of establishing your I Am and your I Am Letting Go statements is providing you with an intentional focus that is more powerful than the ranting and raving of your inner critic.

Initially, expect the voice of your inner critic to react with a barrage of loud and denigrating comments about your new I Am and Letting Go statements.

By claiming ownership of these statements here and now, we are sending an engraved invitation to your inner critic to do its job. The critic is the voice of your reactive mind.

When our life choices are made by our ego, we will never be as good as we think we are or as bad as we think we are. Therefore, we will use our creative energy to try to win arguments with our inner critic and our critic will always have the upper hand.

We will delve further into the identity of this pesky troublemaker later on. All you need to know right now is that from this moment on, there are only two experiences to be on the lookout for:

1.   You will be living in the experiences expressed in your I Am and you will be letting go of the experiences stated in your Letting Go.

This means that your intentions are manifesting and your intuition, intellect, and emotions are all working together for a common purpose.

Or:

2.   You will be living in the experiences expressed in your Letting Go and you will be letting go of the experiences stated in your I Am.

This means that your intellect and/or your emotions got scared or threatened, pushed your intuition out of the driver's seat, and took over to regain control. At this point, your inner critic becomes the co-pilot and your intuition and higher guidance is relegated to the back seat.

To re-establish your I Am and I Am Letting Go statements as your core intent, simply stop. Ask yourself what is right action to move you towards the actualization of your I Am and what is right action to let go of your Letting Go.

Dismiss your inner critic by turning your attention back to your I Am and Letting Go statements of intent.

Your Best Future Self

Now I want you to visualize, *imagine*, that you are standing on a wide path that winds both to the left and to the right, as far as your eyes can see.

Take a few moments to notice as much as you can about your path. Pause here to give yourself time to close your eyes and visualize. Notice whether your particular path seems to be leading you down into a valley, or perhaps it winds up a steep hill or mountain, or something else entirely different.

Also notice the time of year and the time of day and the temperature outside. See what kinds of trees…shrubs…grass…or flowers…are growing around or near your particular path. Notice what the path itself looks like. Is it paved or gravel or dirt or something else?

When you are ready, begin to walk on this path. Test it out. See how familiar it feels. Notice if you can walk on it with a free, easy, and graceful pace. Notice as much as you can about how you feel as you walk on this path.

You may find yourself experiencing slight to mild or even fairly strong feelings of apprehension, of not knowing where exactly you are going. Know that these feelings of insecurity may simply be your habitual way of experiencing the beginnings of new expansion. Know that it is possible to replace those feelings with a sense of exhilaration and a strong sense of personal security. But don't take my word for it. Simply stop for a moment on your path and clearly, with intent, call to your Highest and Best Future Self. Simply wait patiently, as you notice your illuminated Future Self coming towards you until your Future Self reaches you and is now standing before you. Pause here, take a deep breath and drink in the imagined vision of your future self.

Take a moment to merge with your Future Self.

⟳ *All that is required of you is deciding to be open*
and receptive to all future possibilities that are
available to you to further your soul growth.

Imagine that your future self turns and faces forward. Simply step into your Highest Future Self and feel the merging of who you are today into who you are destined to become. Take as long as you want as you actually feel your energy expanding.

When you are ready, allow your Future Self to take you on an exploration of your possible futures. Pause for a moment to allow yourself to experience whatever information is there for you at this particular time.

Again, there is nothing for you to do other than to allow your Future Self to share with you, either through a feeling or sensations, thoughts, or visual pictures. Simply know that you will be shown whatever is best for you at this time. Now separate once again from your Future Self and take a deep breath and then let it go and relax back into yourself.

Your Future Self is going to leave you in a moment but first you will be given a specific and special present that symbolizes your best possible future.

⟳ *Simply open your hands in a gesture of receiving*
and you will be given your special symbolic gift.

Take a moment to notice what you have been given. Feel it, sense it, run your hands over it until it makes itself known to you. What is it? What special meaning does it hold for you? And now allow your path to fade and disappear from view.

Take a few moments to write down what you experienced.

You are beginning to establish an active relationship with your intuition through the exercising of your imaginative perception skills. Seeing your best future self is an example of the right use of this skill. Court your intuition and it will partner for life with your intellect as a trusted friend and companion.

We have covered important territory by finding your two symbols, establishing your first I Am and Letting Go statements, and introducing a beginning intention to take the power out of the hands of your reactive mind/inner critic.

You have also experienced making an energetic connection with your Best Future Self and been given a symbolic present that represents your best possible future.

This might be a good place to rest, relax your focus, validate your accomplishments, and give yourself time to integrate these new experiences.

When you feel ready, willing, and able, we will resume our journey ahead.

CHAPTER 3   COURTING INTUITION

Imagine that you have decided to entice intuition into your life. It is worth courting and is highly sought after because of the many benefits it brings.

It is an expert at discovery, creative problem solving, and decision-making. It is a masterful generator of ideas, a forecaster and a revealer of truths. It is a skilled and subtle guide to successful living.

It brings another way to use our minds and to approach knowledge. It gives us access to understanding who we are and what we need, and it allows us to move toward the realization of our highest potential.

It sits ready and willing to contribute its gifts to the person who is willing to create an environment in which it can thrive.

If you believe in intuition's talents and abilities intellectually yet at the same time harbor mistrust on an emotional level, your intuition will be a hesitant and inconsistent contributor to your life.

Intuition flourishes in an environment of self-trust and conceptual and behavioral flexibility.

Here is a quick sketch of four important attitudes and behaviors to cultivate if you want to get intuition's attention. We will delve deeper into these four components when we talk about self-trust.

1. The first necessary ingredient to entice intuition into your life is congruence. This means being willing to uncover and discover our needs, establish our core values, and have our thoughts and feelings working together on the same

team so that our behavior is aligned with who we are and what we stand for. It is the ability to walk our talk, to say yes when we mean yes and no when we mean no because we have taken the time to discern what is important to us. When we are incongruent, we say yes when we mean no and no when we mean yes and therefore have very little personal power at our command.

2. The second behavior is reliability. We do what we say we will do. We make agreements with ourselves and we honor them. We take ownership of the responsibility for our lives.

3. The third behavior is openness. Openness is the willingness to examine our preconceived ideas about who we are, what we think, and how we feel. It is the skill of intellectual and emotional curiosity about ourselves. The opposite behavior is a *don't confuse me with the facts* attitude.

4. The fourth is acceptance. Acceptance is the willingness to accept all aspects of ourselves, both the positive and the negative, without judging ourselves harshly, even if we don't like what we find. Acceptance is the ability to treat ourselves with respect and a healthy positive regard.

Congruence, reliability, openness, and acceptance are the four pillars that create self-trust. Most of us find at least one of these four components troublesome.

When you commit to increasing your effectiveness in that one neglected area, your self-trust will begin to expand and your intuition will instantly become more easily available to you.

Anti-Intuitive Behaviors

In order to get intuition's full cooperation, here are attitudes and behaviors that intuition finds particularly unappealing. They need to be addressed before your intuition will give you a second glance.

We will call these anti-intuitive behaviors.

1. The first is low self-esteem. Intuition isn't attracted because low self-esteem often translates into a serious mistrust of anything that comes from within ourselves.

2. Next in line is a fear of success. Intuition likes to help make things work through creative, imaginative, and innovative solutions. When we expect to fail, we are closed to hearing the intuitive messages that would assist in having our decision-making work.

3. A lack of confidence and lack of permission to think independently will keep us from opening to our intuition because of the discomfort with the often surprising, unpredictable, and unconventional knowledge that is available to us from our own unique wisdom base.

4. Living in the fast lane keeps us too distracted, keeps us numb to our deeper needs and desires, and keeps us out of touch with the ability to hear the subtleties and nuances that is the language that intuition speaks.

5. Excessive security needs, fear of change, and intolerance of uncertainty all conspire to stifle and suffocate intuition's gifts. When we seek control and predictability over our lives by the following of rigid rules, our intuition gets limited to safety issues rather than being valued for its strongest talents, which are innovation and creativity.

6. When we take our work, our problems, our lives, and ourselves too seriously we create a climate that kills spontaneity. Intuition and humor are cousins. They have in common the ability to take wild, unexpected illogical leaps in thinking that can be both practical and entertaining. But neither can survive in a climate devoid of light, expectant energy.

As we continue to glean more knowledge about our current relationship with these attitudes and behaviors, we will free ourselves from stagnant, false, and dead-end self-doubt and confusion.

> *Our ability to choose right action steps will be en-*
> *hanced as we learn to anticipate the twists and*
> *turns of the path through the maze of life choices*
> *we are continuously asked to make.*

Your intuitive knowledge, when in partnership with your intellect, will allow you to easily and effectively create a life that is solidly grounded and fed by your own unique storehouse of wisdom.

Self-Trust

Self-trust is the container through which intuition speaks. Learning to trust our intuitive wisdom is based upon the ability to create the paradoxical climate of protective boundaries and receptivity to the clues that surface all around us regarding the people and situations with which we interact.

Trust is confidence, reliance, faith, belief, hope, expectation, and assured anticipation. If we break trust down into understandable behaviors, we can begin to make sense of how we can become skilled trust-builders in our relationships with first ourselves and then, through an extension of those skills, to others.

The motivation to know ourselves is the starting point. Self-knowledge comes from direct perception, acquaintance with experience, information, and understanding of our strengths and weaknesses.

> *Self-knowledge can come only through our will-*
> *ingness to participate fully in the game of life.*

When we come to the decision to author our own lives, self-trust becomes the foundation that underlies what we move toward and include and what we turn away from. Our ability to successfully choose what to say yes to and what to say no to increases our ability to trust ourselves.

The foundation for building healthy relationships is the ability to foster trust through our interactions with others. We either build or diminish trust by our intentions and behaviors.

It is important to become aware of the components of high-level human relating and to discover where our strengths lie and which behaviors need to be embraced in order to expand our ability to be trust-builders.

Of course, honesty must be present as a basic intent. The willingness to be genuine is the framework on which the rest of the behaviors are built.

Let's break down the components of trust into four specific categories.

Reliability

Reliability is the ability to do what we say we will do. It requires that we commit ourselves to take specific actions and to follow through on those actions to completion or to renegotiate the commitment if we find that we are going in the wrong direction. The first cornerstone of trust building is reliability.

PERFORMABLE BEHAVIORS THAT ENHANCE RELIABILITY:

1. I do what I say I will do.

2. I am on time for appointments.

3. I make sure I fully understand what is expected of me before I take on a commitment or project.

4. I make agreements and keep them.

5. If I cannot keep an agreement, I take responsibility to renegotiate.

6. I refer to an appointment book or calendar before I commit to an obligation.

7. I can be counted on to show up prepared to participate.

8. I am aware of my limitations and strengths and consider both when I am asked to take on a task.

9. I follow through from beginning to end when I commit to a project.

10. I take initiative over a wide variety of ways of relating to others and I am willing to take ownership of the outcomes of my interactions.

Congruence

Next comes congruence. We are congruent personally when our needs, our values, our thoughts, our feelings, and our actions are aligned and consistent. We say yes when we mean yes and no when we mean no. Our energies all line up in the same direction. We are 'all of one fabric.'

Conversely, when we say yes and we really mean no or no when we really mean yes, we create static in our nervous system. Our personal music starts hitting sour notes. When our yesses and no's are at odds, we experience doubt and confusion and begin to mistrust our own signals.

PERFORMABLE BEHAVIORS THAT ENHANCE CONGRUENCE:

1. I say yes when I mean yes and no when I mean no.

2. When I talk with others, I am clear and specific, not vague and general.

3. I deal with concrete experience and behavior when I talk.

4. I provide a lot of detail when I talk because details make a message clear and understandable.

5. I am direct and use my directness as a way to get involved with others.

6. I know where I stand with others and they know where they stand with me because I am willing to express both my thoughts and my feelings.

7. My facial expressions and body language express the same as my words.

8. I communicate responsibly and with care and use my directness to connect with others rather than to dominate or punish.

9. Being sincere and genuine is very important to me.

10. I send out the same message through my feelings, my thoughts, and my behaviors.

It would seem that we could stop at reliability and congruence, and having mastered these two skills, we would be secure and protected from further self-doubt and confusion since we would know who we are and also exactly what we are doing.

If life were static, unchanging, and predictable we could stop here.

Life, however, is active, dynamic, unpredictable, and ever-changing. Therefore, our next challenge is to court the dual skills of appropriate openness and acceptance of the quirks and missteps of ourselves and others. Life requires that we bend, flex, and stretch.

Openness

Openness is the ability to allow others entrance into the secret and hidden chambers of our inner life. It requires discernment and risk. Vulnerability and visibility. It carries no guarantee that we will be understood or that the results of our openness will be predictable or controllable.

Openness is tricky business. Say too much and you may be setting yourself up for unpredictable outcomes. Stay closed and you may cut yourself off from the wellspring of vibrant, intriguing, surprising, and precious intimacy and the climate that fosters newly formed and deeper interpersonal connections and new understandings.

PERFORMABLE BEHAVIORS THAT ENHANCE OPENNESS:

1. I use self-disclosure to help establish sound relationships with others.

2. I am willing to disclose my thoughts and feelings. I let others know the 'person inside.'

3. I am willing to feel visible and vulnerable.

4. I am open without being a secret revealer or an exhibitionist.

5. I am genuine and authentic in my interactions.

6. I rely on my identity or personal power more than my role or position to influence outcomes.

7. I am comfortable with maintaining eye contact when talking with others.

8. I use a smile or touch as effectively as words in establishing a connection with others.

9. I am able to say, "I don't know" when I am asked for information outside of my knowledge base.

10. I can acknowledge mistakes. I allow myself to be "real" rather than "perfect."

Acceptance

Acceptance is the ability to express as well as feel a willingness to embrace all the unique aspects of another. Self-acceptance is the ability to accept all our incongruent and out-of-sync quirks and insecurities as well as our strengths and innate gifts.

PERFORMABLE BEHAVIORS THAT ENHANCE ACCEPTANCE:

1. I express in a variety of ways that I am "for" others and respect them.

2. I attempt to see the world through the eyes of others. I put myself inside their skin (empathy).

3. I listen well to both verbal and non-verbal cues and ask for clarification when I get mixed signals.

4. I am able to hear the whole message of others, even when I disagree with their opinions or beliefs.

5. I am able to express my opinions and feelings with authority figures.

6. I actively accept others even when I do not necessarily agree with them.

7. I speak my truth and listen intently to others so I can understand what is true for them.

8. I am non-defensive in my interactions with others.

9. I avoid comparing myself to others. I value my uniqueness and enjoy learning about others.

10. I believe all persons have an innate capability to find solutions and manage their own lives.

Openness and acceptance are spurred on by positive curiosity about the vastness inherent in what we don't know about ourselves and others.

Openness and acceptance combine to generate enthusiasm for the unfolding, unpredictable and adventurous jolts that come from life.

Enthusiasm is the divine particle in this composition of trust that allows us to fashion our lives from all that is great, generous, and true.

Without it, we are constantly in danger of squandering our precious life energy trying to keep our lives predictable and keeping ourselves small-minded, closed-hearted, false, and mean-spirited.

None of us wants to see ourselves as trust diminishers. You may even perceive trust building as one of your well-developed skills.

However, when we look closely, we find that we tend to surround ourselves with people who have our same strengths and actually avoid or feel uncomfortable with people who have our under-developed traits as their strengths.

It is helpful to know that a person who scores high in openness can be judged as inconsistent and out of control by a more closed person.

A more critical person can judge someone who is skilled in acceptance as being gullible and willing to accept mediocre performance.

Someone who has a hard time saying no can evaluate a person who is versed in congruent behaviors as being blunt and cold.

And a person who scores high in reliability can be seen as being too serious and boring by a person who has a difficulty making commitments.

You can begin to increase your ability to be more flexible in your personal and professional relationships when you can recognize your own and others' developed and under-developed traits. You can use your knowledge of the four categories of reliability, congruence, openness, and acceptance to bring about cooperation, respect for diversity, and enhanced interpersonal effectiveness.

It is particularly useful to be aware of your under-developed traits. That knowledge can be used to effectively analyze situations that are not turning out the way you hoped. Practice performing the new behaviors you have pinpointed and you will find that interpersonal conflicts can be resolved easily and more effectively.

Trust-building is an art, not a science. High competency in these trust-building behaviors brings great rewards. What is not so obvious about these four categories is that they are extremely important to your relationship with yourself.

Are you open and honest with yourself? Are you accepting of yourself? Are your needs, your values, your thoughts, your feelings, and your behaviors congruent? Do you keep your commitments to yourself?

Your relationship with these components determines your individual self-trust quotient. When you increase your competency in these four areas, you will be rewarded with immediate results in enhanced self-regard and inner solidity.

Success and Fulfillment

There is a jump rope game that young girls play called 'Double Dutch'. It requires two ropes of the same length and two people holding both ends of both the ropes in their left and right hands. Each rope is turned towards the middle, one after the other.

The object of the game is to have a line of players jump in and out of both ropes without getting tripped up in either rope. The hardest part of the game is to decide exactly the right moment to jump in. Ready, set...wait a minute. One...two...not just yet.

Once you are in, all it takes is steady rhythmic jumping in tune with the two simultaneously turning ropes. Double Dutch requires awareness, intention, heightened attention, discerning decision-making capabilities, coordination, and a sense of rhythm, timing and tempo.

Living life wholeheartedly takes the same skills.

When we have a purpose bigger than our moment-to-moment thoughts and feelings, the game begins. We mobilize our efforts towards the achievement of our external goals. Actualizing goals creates the experience of success.

Success is rope number one. Identifying our top values, solidifying what integrity and authenticity means to us, and uncovering and discovering our unique rhythm, timing, and tempo creates a climate of fullness and richness. Openness, honesty, acceptance, congruence between our thoughts and feelings, and reliability are some of the basic attributes of authenticity. Authenticity fleshes out success. Fulfillment is the result.

Fulfillment is rope number two. When we have access to our 'make it happen' energy, we bring the principle of healthy, productive masculine energy into our lives. When we loosen our tight grip of control by acknowledging our use of 'not knowing' the answer, the direction, the next step, we get out of our own way enough to begin the process of acknowledging, accepting, allowing, and trusting the serendipitous gifts of the Universe.

The rhythmic cadence that is created between going after life and welcoming life as a beloved friend who has come to visit, sets the stage for a full, rich partnership with our highest and best self.

When our sights are firmly set on the North Star of success and we spend all of our energies lusting after outcomes, we are destined to experience life as a one-dimensional, single-minded, single-loop game.

When we stay forever seated in predictable comfort, safety, and security, and an unwillingness to venture out into unknown territory, we reduce our life script to a few well-rehearsed roles that we play out halfheartedly until boredom and numbness become our steady diet of convenience.

If we abstain from continuing to take a fair-share bite out of life, we have nothing of value to digest that keeps us stimulated and mentally and emotionally alive. Our vibrant life opportunity becomes endangered and reduced down to never-ending reruns of worn-out memories from our shadow past.

The Double Dutch approach to life sets the stage for intuition to come to the party. By asking ourselves some deeper questions, we begin to invite intuition's powers of inspired right action into our lives.

1. Where do I want to invest my time, energy, knowledge, and caring?

2. What principles and values am I willing to uphold?

3. How much of my creative, innovative, 'can-do' energy is held hostage in mummified regrets, resentments, and jealousies, and shortsighted attachment to perceived hurts and injustices?

4. What keeps me stuck on the sidelines?

5. When will it be the right time for me to jump in wholeheartedly?

6. What am I waiting for?

It is important to put the rope-turning job in the hands of our highest spiritual guidance.

The next step is to get ready, set, and jump in to a full, wholehearted partnership between ourselves and our best and highest selves and that force that holds the Universe and us in its hands.

A Sense of Mastery

Imagine that you find yourself traveling along a winding road that is marked by a signpost that identifies it as your unique path of life. You are simultaneously riding two horses, like a circus performer who has mastered the art of standing up with one foot planted on the back of each horse. The horse on the right is called Looking Good and the one on the left is named Feeling Good.

Looking Good and Feeling Good want to work well together. Their task is to learn to synchronize their pacing so that you, the rider, get two main benefits. When they work in partnership you reap the rewards of position power in the world from Looking Good and personal power and inner solidity from Feeling Good.

The problem is that Looking Good has a tendency towards domination and over-control. Looking Good likes the protection of appearing perfect to the external world by always trying to be right, good, smart, stable, 'better than,' and a winner at all times and in as many ways as possible.

Looking Good is always striving for perfection and likes to be the lead horse. Looking Good demands positive accomplishment and is relentless in the pursuit of image management and more, bigger, and better results, no matter what.

Feeling Good is more high-strung and gets fatigued with Looking Good's inability to ever be satisfied with anything. The push for perfection is frantic, anxiety-producing, and all-consuming; sometimes Feeling Good intentionally slows down in silent protest.

When this happens you know it because you begin to be stretched too far and the ride becomes precarious and very uncomfortable.

Feeling Good has dreams of slow, sensuous sauntering down the path on a pristine day, stopping occasionally to nibble clover on the side of the road.

Feeling Good likes to be productive, but also loves variety and loses vitality and zest for living when subjected to Looking Good's constant demands: pushing and prodding to hurry up so that they never fall behind and lose their competitive edge.

Looking Good started out being trained early to be a racehorse. Many years were spent lined up at the starting gate packed in next to all the other horses intent on the same goal. If you didn't win, place, or at least show, you were always in danger of being sold off or overlooked until you were no longer useful and would be put out to pasture.

That thought is unbearable to Looking Good and so, even though there is no race on the Personal Path of Life, Looking Good keeps blinders on while chanting a litany of past accomplishments and future, unfulfilled goals to keep striving, pushing and forging ahead.

Looking Good and Feeling Good have carried you this far. Let's take a moment now to stop and assess the quality of your ride.

Has Looking Good been setting the pace and left Feeling Good in the position of being dragged unhappily forward? Is your Feeling Good horse feeling *very* bad, resentful, stuck, and stopped, with a chronic attitude problem?

It may be time to create a truce between your Looking Good horse and your Feeling Good horse.

1. **Take the reins** and give Looking Good and Feeling Good a renewed purpose that will give them more room to become equal partners in the creation of a smoother, more satisfying ride for you from now on. Reaffirm your I Am and I Am Letting Go statements.

2. **Resolve to let go** of seeing yourself and your life as a never-ending problem to be solved.

3. **Decide to embrace each day** as a new reality to be experienced so that you can practice the art of thriving rather than striving.

4. **Use your feelings** as an internal compass to let you know how Looking Good and Feeling Good are communicating.

5. **Validate** your accomplishments and also learn to pace yourself so that you become acclimated to your own unique and personal rhythm, timing, and tempo.

6. **Wholeheartedly embrace** the worthwhile task of reining in your runaway need for unrealistic perfection while encouraging your feelings to add vitality and emotional sincerity to everything you pursue.

As you learn to be both productive and emotionally solid, your sense of personal mastery will blossom naturally into a strengthened feeling of full, wholehearted involvement and commitment to the quality and not just the quantity of your life.

Wholeheartedness calls us to soften our hold on protective pretenses so that we can surrender into more emotional sincerity.

When we seek to live our lives fully connected to our emotions as well as our intellectual abilities, we are able to bring the whole of ourselves into our relationships, our work, our values, and our accomplishments.

CHAPTER 4   REVITALIZING YOUR SOUL

When my daughter Jennica was about three years old, she came running from her room and buried her head in my lap. "There's a monster in my room!" she said.

"Yikes!" I said, as I snuggled her closer to me. "Monsters aren't allowed in your room. Let's go and tell it to get out."

We held hands and headed down the hall and entered her room. Jennica pointed to the wall and said: "There it is!" There it was. Her little shadow was projected on the wall as big as life.

Jennica was startled by the unexpected. Her little body registered the real-time experience of being frightened and her fight/flight survival response reacted both efficiently and effectively.

Startled is the wake-up call, frightened is the body response, and fear is the result. What an incredible system we each inherit at birth to assist us in the job of survival.

How is it then, that fear has gotten such a bad rap? The best explanation of what fear is comes from Joseph Chilton Pearce, who wrote *The Crack in the Cosmic Egg* back in the 1970s.

A summary of his take on fear is this: There is only startled and frightened. They are real experiences that happen in our body. Everything else is manufactured in our mind.

Guilt is intellectual fear about what we have done in the past.

Resentment is intellectual fear about what has been done to us in the past.

Hostility is intellectual fear about what is currently happening to us.

Anxiety is intellectual fear about what might happen to us in the future.

Given that, doesn't it make sense to take all that intellectual power and invest it in establishing a purpose bigger than our moment-to-moment random thoughts and feelings?

Establishing a full partnership with our intuitive guidance allows the dawning of a new day. We can then set about the business of welcoming our orphaned, startled, and frightened feelings from the past back home.

They can finally rest their head in our lap and tell us: "There was a monster in my room!" There was. Our startled feelings were real. We survived. Now we are safe and secure enough to permit ourselves to thrive.

Finishing Unfinished Business

Imagine that we could be reborn and this time we would show up fully formed with all the learning from our life experiences and none of the unfinished business and unclaimed heart-hurts that we suffered while growing up.

Imagine further that as a result, we would find ourselves connected and solidly grounded in our core, personal power. We would fully own and have command of our talents, would clearly know our preferences, and be able to access our inner wisdom and intuitive guidance as we choose what we say yes to and what requires a no.

- We would be genuine, authentic, all of one fabric, and fully ready, willing, and able to confidently access our storehouse of knowledge, wisdom, and creative energy that would generate our full, rich participation in the creation of our lives.

- We would be visible and vulnerable, porous, unarmored, and curious; open and receptive rather than defensive, hyper-vigilant, and self-critical.

- We would be able to connect with others in the spirit of communion, creating understanding by seeking out ways in which we are similar and allowing our differences to be put on the back burner.

- We would also be able to interact with people who hold a different set of values and realities and be willing to use those differences to expand our knowledge base.

We would have no need to feel threatened by differences or driven to invalidate and make another wrong because they disagree with our point of view. We would have enough inner solidity to agree to disagree.

We wouldn't be threatened, jealous, envious, or resentful of anyone because we would be exquisitely aware that we are walking on our one-of-a-kind life path and are happy and fulfilled because we are clear that we are not in competition with anyone.

I asked you to entertain this imagining because it points to the fact that it is impossible to unleash the power of our intuition until we have established a core connection with the essence of who we are.

Underneath who we pretend to be sits layers of thoughts and feelings. These misconceptions, unexpressed heart-hurts, abandonments, embarrassments, shame, rage, anger, guilt, and resentments could be categorized under the title *who we are afraid we are.*

Sitting underneath who we pretend to be sits who we are afraid we are. Underneath who we are afraid we are is the inner core circle that houses who we are—our essence qualities.

When we are willing to let go of the pretense of being better than or less than, we can take on the task of courageously facing our fears. As we learn to welcome our rejected emotions home so that the heart wounds of our past can finally begin to heal, we will be rewarded with a growing connection to the essence of who we are.

Make a Run for It

So many of us are incarcerated in a mental and emotional prison. This prison comprises solid, thick bricks fashioned from our perceived mistakes, guilts, regrets, heart-hurts, resentments, and self-condemnation.

The mortar that solidly holds the prison walls in place is formed by harsh judgments from significant others, whether persons or institutions, who we imbued with power and authority over our intrinsic self-worth.

The job of dismantling the entire structure is so daunting and overwhelming that most of us prefer to serve our life sentence resigned to sleeping away our time in a numbed-out fog of resignation.

Instead of planning our escape, we use our power of thought to conjure up plausible justifications for where we find ourselves.

We were framed. It is unfair. We got too harsh a sentence. We had a bad defense due to incompetent representation. The judge and jury wouldn't give us a break. We are among the unfortunate ones who never had the right opportunities. If we were more privileged or better connected we would not be in this situation. No wonder we can sometimes struggle under a cloud of depression and hopelessness.

Take heart. If we are willing to give up the unrealistic expectation that it is necessary to remove every brick before we can be free, the task becomes more manageable. All we need to do is tunnel an escape route from our individual cells.

The opening just needs to be big enough to see the light of day and allow us to squeeze through the opening and out into the wide-open freedom of the unknown that lies beyond the prison walls.

Here come the stumbling blocks to freedom that must be confronted in order to proceed.

1. The first is giving up lusting after perfection. "Once I figure out everything that made me feel inferior, bad, wrong, and powerless then I will fix it all and take my rightful place in the world as superior, good, right, and powerful. That will assure me of living happily ever after."

Don't be too quick to dismiss this state of mind as one that you don't carry. Behind every hasty decision that brought unforeseen consequences is usually the faulty notion that we can land on the one right decision that will yield all benefits and demand no prices.

2. When we are too focused on outcomes while ignoring the step-by-step process of getting there, we create a life that is distasteful to our soul and devoid of nourishment on a daily basis. It is like approaching eating as though we can somehow find the meal that will allow us to eat once and for all.

Most of us carry our particular prison with us like a turtle encased in its shell. The benefits are many. Safety, security, familiarity, predictability, surety, the illusion of control, and protection from outside harm are just a few of the seductions that lure us into treating our lives with indifference.

3. If your spirit is calling to you through the voice of discontent, sadness, frustration, irritation, or disappointment, take heart. Instead of judging these messenger feelings, move in closer and don't be afraid. Revive your curiosity. Ask this heavy-heartedness to reveal its hidden secrets.

What new future is calling to you? What winds of change are beginning to blow? What images and shapes are being formed by your clouds of discontent? Peer into your future on the wings of your present disillusionment.

Bring these furtive glimpses of your future into the present. If you are willing to take responsibility for creating a real, one-of-a-kind, handmade life grown out of your deepest intentions, it is necessary to start small.

Listen to your internal weather report.

Count the beats between the rumbling thunders from ingested injustices.

Celebrate the lightning strikes that illuminate your new path.

Revel in the relief of allowing the rain to wash away closeted heart-hurts and quench the thirst of a parched and restricted soul.

Stand out in the rays of the sun and drink in its power to illuminate your heart.

Wholehearted, one-hundred percent participation in the life you presently have is the key that will unlock the power necessary to pursue your personal freedom, one inspired step at a time.

Low Self-Esteem: Your Inner Critic

One of the major stumbling blocks to trusting your intuition is the voice of your inner critic that we touched on after establishing your I Am and I Am Letting Go statements. Most of us have an inner critic that bombards us with a running commentary on everything we do. We aren't good enough, smart enough, productive enough, motivated enough. We're stupid, selfish, unthinking, and unfeeling. We embarrass ourselves, doubt ourselves, and berate ourselves for any perceived mistakes.

A great deal of chaos occurs in our world because we do not appreciate ourselves and haven't truly considered the importance of developing an attitude of generosity, gentleness, or forgiveness with ourselves. As a result, we become incapable of experiencing inner harmony or peace.

Instead of appreciating our lives, we often take our existence for granted or we criticize ourselves into feelings of depression and hopelessness.

When we frame our lives with unrealistic expectations of perfection, we are constantly driven to the brink of emotional disaster through an internal cacophony of complaints and judgments about our problems and perceived inefficiencies.

Ultimately, we have to accept personal responsibility for uplifting our lives.

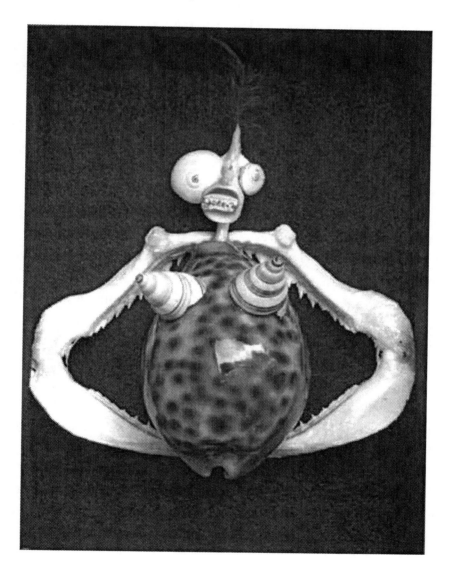

When we stop punishing and condemning ourselves, we can begin to relax and open the window of appreciation. Let the light of appreciation dawn. Then we can begin to contact and connect with the fundamental ground of basic goodness that resides within.

It is extremely important to be willing to open up to ourselves. Developing tenderness towards your life allows you to see both your problems and your potential accurately.

I can hear you now. "That makes sense. Open up to myself. Hear my inner wisdom. Right. As soon as I can win the current argument with my inner critic and prove that I'm right, I'll start on this appreciation thing."

It is important to understand that you will never win an argument with your inner critic. Give it up. You will never convince your critic to retire. It has no scruples and knows everything about you and its only job is to manage you through criticism so you will stay in line.

Let's approach this another way. The reactive mind is a comparative tool. Better than, less than. Nothing is ever enough. In the realm of the ego, we will never be as good as we think we are or as bad as we think we are. The critic is the voice of our reactive mind. It thinks it is keeping us safe from ego damage and external criticism by keeping us informed, up to the minute, on whether we are right or wrong, good or bad, and winning or losing.

Take time off and it says you're lazy. Take on more and it decides you are compulsive. Gain weight and it says you are hopelessly undisciplined. Lose weight and you are vain. Congratulate yourself and you are egotistical. Be fun-loving and you are shallow. Be serious and you are boring. On and on the dialogue goes.

So, how do you take control of this inner monster? Explaining and justifying your position will not work. Quieting the inner critic can only be accomplished through tenderness, gentleness, and humor.

Instead of fighting or ignoring your critic, listen to what it has to say. Take the input. Thank it for sharing. Acknowledge its point of view. Then take your power of choice out of the hands of your critic. Refocus on your current I Am and I Am Letting Go statements. Once you are consciously connected to these two core intentions, exercise your right to choose what is the right action for you.

If you need to question yourself, focus on some deeper issues. Are you doing the best you can given the circumstances you find yourself in? Do you have an internal value system that you are willing to live by?

Are you living in accordance with your own integrity? Are you willing to allow yourself to be satisfied with who you are at this moment? Do you have the courage to be your own authority? Are you staying weak and irresponsible for your happiness? Do you allow other people to relentlessly criticize you as a way to make believe that your life would be terrific if only 'they' would treat you better?

If you are consistently downtrodden, decide to uncurl from the fetal position, stretch your legs, and stand up. Take small steps. Flex your emotional muscles. Move at your own pace. Let what you are doing be enough. Decide to let yourself off the hook. Take a deep breath, relax, let go, and lighten up.

Be willing to listen to your critic and then take the reins of responsibility for being your own authority. Allow your critic to be part of your inquiry but do not allow it to hold an inquisition. You will find your core ability to manage your life strengthening over time.

Self-trust comes in small, steady increments through patience, kindness, and your willingness to take ownership of your right to make your own life choices.

Instead of making your choices based on whether you like to do something or not, ask these two important questions instead. Can you take the reins of your life? More importantly, will you?

If you can answer yes to these two questions, and are connected to your I Am and I Am Letting Go statements, you are on your way to setting your feet firmly on your unique life path, one courageous and strengthening step at a time.

Fear of Success: Breaking the Pattern of Disrespect

Years ago I heard a very articulate and generous Holocaust survivor in her late seventies share her intimate story. "They pushed us. They constantly rushed us. They never let up pushing, yelling and always rushing us. They never let us alone. They never let us slow down."

That thought has stayed with me, bringing the realization that hurrying someone, including hurrying myself, may be the first step in setting up a pattern of disrespect.

When you decide you are not moving fast enough, your production isn't big enough, or your success isn't coming soon enough, discontent takes hold.

On the heels of discontent comes dissatisfaction, irritation, and impatience; then you are just a short step away from fault-finding, self-denigration, and abusive self-criticism.

The accumulation of external messages to hurry up, move it along, be more, do more, and have more can become internalized and take over as a false drive that is relentless and counter-productive.

A healthy motivation is a natural by-product of being involved in work, relationships, and play that we enjoy.

When we spend too much of our time over-viewing our lives, looking over our shoulder to see who or what is out to get us, over-strategizing and planning our future, or dramatizing our past, then something is wrong.

When we unconsciously hold a belief, whether inherited from external sources or because of a conclusion that we drew ourselves, that we deserve to be humiliated and punished, we will treat ourselves on some level the same way the soldiers treat the enemy.

When we find our self-motivation is coming from the end of an invisible whip cracking with self-denigrating judgments about our inadequacies, it is time to stop and re-evaluate our core beliefs.

The decision to thrive begins with a disciplined commitment to let go of the habit of allowing our inner critic, dressed in an army uniform, to berate, denigrate, push, and prod us as we helplessly falter under the pressure.

Thriving can become a real possibility when we begin to cultivate a level of self-knowledge that grows from a sincere desire to become aware of and attentive to our genuine needs, wants, desires, dreams, and passions.

As we gather the strength to become self-supporting and self-validating, we expand our ability to turn away from self-abuse in favor of cultivating the freedom to live in harmony with the highest and best within us.

Lack of Confidence: All Show?

Many of us are suffering from a malady that is widespread but seldom mentioned. It is particularly prevalent among successful, accomplished professionals, both men and women, single or married.

This hidden problem is responsible for lowered motivation, moodiness, and mental and emotional unclarity. It often leads to a feeling of "what's the use."

It is a cousin of loneliness but it has distinct features of its own. It is the deep-seated, unfulfilled need to be truly seen, heard, and understood by another.

When we ignore our need to be accepted in favor of identifying ourselves as being strong and independent, and a man or woman with a mission, we slowly begin to create a split between our thoughts and feelings.

We build an image of ourselves through high-minded thinking while distancing from our fears and apprehensions until they are buried out of sight and out of mind.

At first it *seems* prudent to hold a strong discipline over our fears and the emotional roller coaster that can come from listening too earnestly to them.

In our quest for more, bigger, and better results, however, we can get caught up in pretending to be better than we are and then investing all our energy in promoting that pretense.

Here is the difficulty that arises: **Underneath who we pretend to be lives who we are afraid we are.** When we habitually run from squarely addressing our fears, we begin to lose touch with some of the subtler but extremely important aspects of being authentic and real.

We take ourselves far too seriously. We lose the ability to laugh at ourselves. We keep our distance from everyone by never allowing ourselves to come down, let down, open up, or disclose what isn't working for us.

Image-building and the maintenance of it requires vigilance and a constant shoring up of that image by analyzing what is good, bad, right, or wrong and how to figure it all out and fix it fast so that the performance goes on as usual.

> *An antidote to living an isolated, image-driven existence is to foster the ability to debrief often, with at least one trusted person.*

There is an inexpressible comfort in feeling safe enough to neither have to weigh your thoughts or measure your words in the presence of another.

When you can pour out everything in whatever order it comes and know that you are being received and accepted, the dragons and demons of the mind have an opportunity to be freed from the dungeon within. The inner recesses of your mind can clear and be renewed and restored to health and vitality.

At the heart of true self-worth and authenticity is the knowledge that we are lovable without having to qualify for that acceptance. We need each other to mirror back, as one conscious being to another, that we are seen, heard, and accepted.

The cultivation of the dual values of kindness and acceptance given freely to others has profound rewards. We begin to allow a more graceful and easy self-management style to take root within us.

Our intention is fueled by a warmer and softer approach to our affairs, our lives, and ourselves. We begin to discover that too much brilliance has its disadvantages.

Being the smartest, quickest, and wittiest may raise a laugh in a crowd but often beheads budding trust in friendships that could be better cultivated through quiet acceptance, inviting warmth, and generous doses of kindness.

Living Life in the Fast Lane: Lusting After Outcomes

If we could connect our brains to a loudspeaker and our inner dialogue were projected outward, the noise would be deafening.

Most of us walk around with our creative energy held captive; imprisoned by the demands and commands to hurry up, push through, finish up, do more, be more, and have more.

This cacophony of harsh judgments and negative evaluations is at the root of habitual self-disrespect.

When we decide we are not moving fast enough or our production isn't enough or our success isn't coming fast enough, discontent sets in. Next come dissatisfaction, irritation, and impatience, and then we are just a short step away from self-denigration and self-abuse.

Remember how it felt as a child being totally involved in play, lost in the moment, only to be shocked back into reality by a command or demand that you stop what you were doing and hurry up and…whatever was on your parent's or another authoritative adult's timeline?

The capacity to let go, enough to get totally lost in the experience of the moment, usually leaves us at a young age. We replace it with hyper-vigilant over-viewing, watching out for who is out to get us, over-strategizing, rehearsing, and planning future events, while the power of the present slips away, unnoticed and unused.

The more negative our prodding and pushing is, the more acclimated we become to accepting humiliation and punishment as our habitual way of motivating ourselves.

In order to change our mode of operation from negative to positive, from harsh and judgmental to graceful and easy, we must shift our focus from striving to thriving.

The Courage to Thrive

Thriving requires a 180-degree shift in the way we see events.

Imagine for a moment that who you are right now, where you are, and how you behave is absolutely perfect. There is nothing to fix or figure out about you or anyone around you. Everything is perfect exactly how it is. Therefore your only job is to notice specifically *how* it's perfect.

There is no longer any need for either internal or external dialogues that start with "If only, When, I have to, I should, You have to, You should, It isn't enough, I'm not enough, or You're not enough." Your world is perfect just the way it is and everyone in your life is perfect also.

This isn't a Pollyanna notion. If you are willing to take it to heart, it can ease up a lot of unnecessary tension, irritation, and frustration for you.

When I was still raising my children and also doing seminars, one of my major frustrations was that I would travel away from my family and present five-day intensive workshops, only to come back to an upside-down household.

No matter how much I planned, commanded, and demanded that my husband and children respect the program I carefully laid out, it always turned out the same way. I would go grocery shopping, preplan meals, clean the house, do the laundry, and schedule babysitters so that everything would run smoothly while I was gone.

No matter how well I did this, I would come home to some level of upheaval and upset. I would be exhausted from my work only to be confronted with more demands on my energy and time so that I couldn't relax and let down.

Instead of coming home and catching up on all the things the girls were doing and re-connecting with them and my husband, I would be resentful and irritated that nobody cared. I would immediately start to do dishes or straighten up while feeling used and abused.

This scene played out endlessly. I felt hopeless and helpless to change it. I wouldn't accept it and I couldn't control it. I was a victim of this circumstance with no way out.

One evening, after another long week away, I was driving home and dreading the inevitable mess that would greet me. I started to brace myself by giving myself a lecture about just ignoring the house and focusing on being happy to be home with my family.

"Yes, but it isn't fair that none of them care enough to pick up after themselves." The internal dialogue had begun.

Since high-mindedness often permeates the environment in personal growth seminars, some of it was still hovering around me as I reentered my 'regular' life.

"What if you decide that it is perfect exactly the way it is?"

"I would be lying."

"Think a bit deeper. What would you do or not do if you truly accepted this as just the way it is and not your concern?"

"Well, I can't stand the mess and I want to come down from this intense focus I've been holding for five days. I want to relax in an environment that is quiet and soothing. That's why I am so disappointed when everything is in an upheaval when I get home."

"Why is that?"

"Well, I guess I feel that it is really my responsibility to maintain order in the house and so I feel guilty when I am away. I don't really feel I have any right to demand their cooperation. Then I feel hurt that they don't straighten up before I get home. I take it as a message that they don't care about me."

"So if everything were perfect when you got home, how would you react differently?"

"I would be happy to let them be and I could just get relaxed myself."

"So, what is stopping you from feeling that way yourself now?"

By that time I was driving into the driveway. I went into the house, hugged and kissed my girls, hugged and kissed my husband, looked around and noticed that the house was a mess. I asked if they had eaten the dinner I left for them and they laughed and said that they were too busy all snuggled up watching a movie so they just ate chips…and M&M's.

This time, I tried a new response. "I am so glad to be finished with my work. I am tired and tense so I am going to change my clothes, take a walk down to the beach, and relax a little bit by myself before I catch up on what has been going on with all of you." They thought that was a great idea.

I was gone for about an hour. I sat with a glass of wine, watched the ocean, and allowed me to catch up with me. Then I was ready to go home. When I got there I was greeted with five happy people who were glad to see me. They had even straightened up the house, as an extra miracle.

When I stopped lusting after outcomes by negatively pushing and prodding, life in all its perfection came to me bearing gifts of grace and ease.

Excessive Security Needs: Over-Control Through Self-Harassment

If I asked you to take a piece of paper and quickly write down a list of your current worries, followed by a list of past experiences that you are suffering over, I bet you would surprise yourself with the unconscious mental debris that would quickly float to the surface.

For many of us, worry and suffering are unacknowledged hitchhikers that keep us secured to a treadmill of fear and apprehension about our ability to survive.

In the original form of the word 'worry' someone else is doing the harassing, strangling, or choking. Therefore, to worry oneself is a form of self-harassment.

Let's take a look at why worry and suffering are common ways we may be misusing our mental and emotional energies.

For example, worry can be used to avoid change. When we worry, we obsessively focus on our problems and by doing that we manufacture fear instead of shifting our focus to find solutions. Our fear amplifies while we continue to avoid doing anything about the matters at hand.

Worry may serve as a way to avoid admitting that we are powerless over something. Rather than surrendering to the temporary insecurity of the unknown, unknowable, and unfixable, at least worry makes us feel like we are doing something.

Worry is often a family inheritance passed down from generation to generation as an unexamined belief that to worry about someone shows love. The other side of this belief is that not worrying about someone means that you don't care about them. Worry becomes a way to appear invested in someone's well-being without really being involved.

If I worry about you, frantically treat you like a fix-it project, try to figure you out, push you, prod you, and overwork your life, I can conveniently avoid taking action in my own life. I can use mental gymnastics to distance myself from the discomfort of witnessing and feeling your pain and fear that might trigger my own unacknowledged fear and pain.

Pain and fear are necessary and valuable components of life. Suffering and worry are destructive and unnecessary exaggerations of authentic pain and fear.

Worrying and long-term suffering are two extremely stubborn habits that keep us locked onto the victim seesaw of limited emotional expression called sad and mad.

Habitual worrying and chronic suffering are clever disguises of the runaway ego that can never be satisfied. From the ego's point of view, we will never be as good as we think we are and we will never be as bad as we think we are.

We can stop this unproductive self-harassment by taking a moment to stop, look, and choose a deeper relationship with our intuitive guidance.

⌐⎯⎯ *Bring your I Am and I Am Letting Go statements back into focus now.*

When we center ourselves in the knowledge of our basic goodness and the basic goodness of our lives, we affirm once again that life is to live, that love is there, that nothing is a promise but that beauty exists and when sought after it magically appears and that happily ever after comes one precious moment and one right action at a time.

Fear of Changing: Growing and Progressing

The corporation I worked for in the late sixties was very progressive. Even the letterhead was embossed with the words *To grow and progress is to change.*

If we take this statement at face value, "to grow" sounds good, "to progress" sounds positive, and therefore, "to change" should be greeted with open arms also.

What? Do I sense a little hesitation in your enthusiasm for change?

Let's take a closer look. When confronted with change there are two basic responses we can have. We can see change as a threat and respond by fighting or fleeing, or we can view it as an opportunity to respond creatively. The way we respond to change depends on how the change comes about.

Think back on your life. Recall a major change that was generated and controlled by you. How did you feel about it?

Now recall a life change that was thrust upon you and over which you had little or no control. The more *you* felt in control of the changes, the more *you* could orchestrate them, the more positive you probably felt.

Therefore, an important point to remember regarding change is that the more control you have, the easier it is to change and feel positive about that change.

This brings us back to the initial hesitation. Life has a funny habit of forgetting to ask for our two cents before delivering opportunities on our doorsteps.

We get jumpy when asked to change our habits, our behaviors, our affiliations, our jobs, or anything that we comfortably count on, even if we know we need to change. How can we approach change more productively?

First, let's cover some of the basics.

When we are maintaining our comfortable positions, and life unceremoniously comes knocking on our door with something unanticipated, unexpected, or distasteful, our first emotional response to this new challenge will be resistance.

If the situation doesn't go away when we try to reject it, our resistance turns quickly to resentment. As the pressure mounts, our thoughts slide easily into how to get revenge by making shortsighted decisions that often make the situation worse. This is called the emotional maintenance cycle.

Here is an example. Your boss says there is some concern about your results lately and a meeting to review your working strategy would be in order.

You say okay but you feel shot down and invalidated. The resistance begins. You return to your office and you can't even remember what you were planning to do today. All you really want to do is walk out.

"Who does she think she is? She has no idea how much time and effort I've already put in on this impossible project. She's lucky to have any results given the way this company is run. It's through my contacts and my reputation that we've progressed this far…"

The resentment pot is starting to boil. Here comes revenge knocking at the door. Now, blatant revenge tactics are frowned upon in our society. Going postal is not the preferred means of solving disagreements.

Here is where our behavior gets subtle. Sometimes we turn the revenge on ourselves, in the form of making short-term decisions that don't serve us. For example: "If she doesn't see my value, I'm pulling back my efforts. I'm just going to do enough to get by. Why should I go all out if I'm not going to be appreciated? I don't want to start all over somewhere new but maybe I had better cover my bases. I'll avoid her and start looking for a new job. Why waste my time in this go-nowhere situation?"

The good news is you haven't shot your boss. The bad news is you are starting to shoot yourself in the foot.

Your boss may be simply asking for more input and more inclusion in the project. Perhaps she is missing data that will ultimately secure your position or even elevate your proficiency in her eyes.

Maybe she is just difficult and there is no solution for you but to leave. Proceeding on the revenge trail will keep you from ever finding out the real truth about the situation.

How do you shift your response to new challenges from resistance to seeing change as a real opportunity? The answer is to have a purpose in mind that is bigger than your moment-to-moment thoughts and feelings.

Being resistant, initially, is part of being human.

The call to grow through change rocks our feelings of physical, mental, and emotional safety. When our security is threatened, we react rather than respond.

Here is where the partnership between intuition and intellect comes in.

Back to our example. Asking some deeper questions is crucial to finding new and appropriate creative responses.

What is your purpose in tackling this project in the first place? Are you committed to bringing in the best results? Are you on target with a workable strategy? After reviewing where you are and where you want to be with the project, you can then proceed to formulate your bigger purpose: "I am creating results by building strong relationships with our vendors and making sure our interactions with them are beneficial for all parties. I am committed to meeting our objectives and making sure they get their needs met also."

Now you have a purpose that aligns your values, thoughts, feelings, and behaviors. You are ready to communicate your goals clearly when you meet with your boss. Of course, this is a hypothetical example, but you get the point.

Change can only be navigated creatively when we are standing on solid ground and are focused on what we want instead of cringing in fear of the unknown.

It is important to take the time to get clear on what we want to have happen—the results. But, identifying the external results you want is only the first step.

Next, and most important, ask yourself what the experience is that you want to create. This allows you to start the process of discovering and uncovering what will create emotional satisfaction for you.

In this case, it is establishing mutually beneficial relationships with the vendors, building trust relationships, and using your ability to relate to people in a genuine and productive way.

This is the process of using intuitive vision and external goals together to form an overall purpose.

> *Taking the time to establish clear intentions invites and allows our creativity to participate in the process of change.*

When we elevate our thinking to move beyond the moment-to-moment, small, and petty hurts and slights of life, we find ourselves able to negotiate change through creative responses. This openness to new ways of responding brings the ultimate reward: increased self-trust.

When we put in the time and effort to learn to trust ourselves by setting clear intentions and following through on our highest and best ideals, we begin the process of building an equal partnership with our Higher Power that will serve us well, no matter what challenges life brings our way.

Taking Ourselves Too Seriously: The Right Use of Humor

The business of living authentically rather than perfectly requires the cultivation of a sense of humor.

Living unrehearsed and in the present is a participation sport. It is energetically costly to be awake, aware, responsive, and engaged in our lives.

It is risky to the ego. A run-in with reality can bruise our idealized version of who we think we are. Enough ego bruises and it becomes tempting to lock ourselves into the predictability and consistency of a made-up, idealized image and then wearing it like a suit of armor. The bad news is that armor is cold, hard, and heavy.

Imagine being required to suit up and show up each day wearing armor like the knights of old. See yourself setting out to fight the dragons and demons of your personal reality with your sword, your shield, and your particular family-inherited coat of arms; those habitual, reactive ways of coping.

When protection is the motivating drive, it makes perfect sense to accumulate as much proof as possible that we are good, right, perfect, honorable, able, smart, beautiful, fill-in-the-blank, from the perfection side of the street.

When we approach our lives as serious business, we must stay focused, clear, intentional, strong, productive, proactive, and driven, to secure as much evidence that we are winning and we are right, therefore deserving of the good life.

Here is where humor comes in. When our idealized image of ourselves collides with reality, we are presented with a real opportunity to laugh at ourselves. We are handed a glimpse of the gaping chasm between who we pretend to be and who we are.

We are complex. Our emotions are multiple choice, all clamoring for top-dog position rather than simply one, lone, purebred feeling at a time.

We are multifaceted. We have roles and we are more than our roles. We have thoughts and we are more than our thoughts. We have feelings and we are more than our feelings.

When our sense of self is separate from what we do or what we have, we become more flexible and freer to experiment and consider new and different points of view and ways to approach our lives.

There is nothing wrong with focused intensity. The problem lies in the motivation that drives our actions.

Hypervigilance is simply fear dressed up in honorable clothing. After all, who can fault us for being proactive and productive?

When we allow ourselves a moment to breathe in, let down, let go, stabilize, and turn our attention away from doing and having, we can begin to uncover and discover a deep longing that resides within our soul to create a life that can be infused with more lightness, ease, and joy.

When we partner with our deeper, intuitive urgings, we tap into a wellspring of vitality. When we pry open the lid of seriousness that surrounds our striving after perfection, we can begin to hold the hand of humor.

Instead of becoming foolish, useless, unproductive, weak, silly, and ineffectual, we enter into a vast process of learning. We can use this quiet, subtle information to adjust our actions based on moment-to-moment inspiration.

We lighten, open, and become more curious, porous, and receptive to our natural, unique rhythm, timing, and tempo. We begin to be informed about what brings us happiness, what burdens us, what discourages us, and what delights us.

We open to the subtle messages that let us know when to rest and when to take action. Our intuition lets us know what is the right action, moment to moment, in the present, with lightness, grace, and ease.

Lack of Permission: Resentment

Traveling with most of us on our journey is a companion, a shadow. Though invisible, this companion may be having an influence on the degree of difficulty you may be encountering on your path.

It was birthed quite some time ago. The exact time of its birth was the first time the thought "Hey, that's not fair!" entered into your consciousness. It grew bigger and stronger with the thought "Nobody plays fair!" and reached full adulthood with the conclusion "Life just isn't fair!"

The name of this invisible companion is Resentment. Resentment thinks very highly of you. It believes that you are a superior and principled person and therefore you should have everything you desire: "If only other people would act right, would do the right thing, would support you, would see reality, and would be more principled and trustworthy, then…".

Unfortunately, people don't always cooperate. Therefore, Resentment feels perfectly justified in giving you permission to hold back from one-hundred percent wholehearted participation in your life. Resentment's litany of old hurts and losses fills your head with a constant stream of excuses and complaints that allow you to continue to strive and struggle instead of thrive.

This silent partner laments often that other people who really don't deserve them get the lucky breaks. You, on the other hand, do the right thing and pay dearly for it every time you do. You try not to take short cuts or take advantage of situations and people. No matter how hard you try, life seems to smile on the less deserving, instead of the good, the honest, the upright, the principled. Namely, you.

It is time to fully acknowledge Resentment's presence in your life. This is an important day because you are being given the opportunity to become aware of how much internal havoc this invisible hitchhiker may be creating in your life.

Resentment maintains a detailed account of every time you have been slighted, thwarted, or invalidated and quickly turns those experiences into cherished grudges that take energy to keep fed, alive, and well. Resentment stores these negative experiences and fuels your inner dialogue with clever plans of ways that it is okay for you to resist fully participating in your life.

Resentment feels perfectly justified in creating revenge fantasies where you will triumph over your past defeats, certain people that are difficult, and old negative experiences, and then and only then will you finally be free to live a fully thriving life.

If you are willing to take ownership of old grudges that you have been harboring, resentment will be free to fade and disappear from

your life. Resentment will have served its main purpose, which was to protect you from sinking into despair under the weight of disappointments and heart-hurts that you have experienced in the past because your expectations of what a successful life means were immaturely conceived.

The benefit of seeking out and listening to our heart's intelligence by being open to our hurts, our heartaches, and our unfulfilled hopes and dreams is that we can begin to fashion a new approach, a life fostered by self-knowledge.

When we are willing to discover our deeper needs, establish our core values, and align with a purpose bigger than our ego's moment-to-moment thoughts and feelings, we begin to stand up and face forward on our unique life path. Our higher purpose is currently being expressed through our I Am and I Am Letting Go statements.

When we cultivate a full and rich partnership with our intuitive wisdom, we are rewarded with easy access to the best answers to this key question: "Given what life is presenting, what is right action for me at this time?" and then we give ourselves full permission to act on the answer.

Call a Ceasefire

If the point of power is *in* the present, it would seem that all we have to do to live in the present moment is to make new decisions and choices and continue on down our road of life. Simple. Or maybe not.

Let's imagine that every strong decision we have ever made is still alive and well somewhere in our consciousness. So, in third grade, as an example, you experienced that adults didn't listen to you and therefore you decided to keep your important thoughts and feelings to yourself. In sixth grade, your teacher was confusing and when you told her you didn't understand, she embarrassed you in front of the class.

As a result, you decided from then on to make believe you understood even if you didn't. In high school, your first love betrayed you. You decided that it wasn't a good idea to let yourself care deeply.

On life goes as we continue to have impactful experiences and then make decisions as a result.

Let's imagine further that each time one of these decisions is made, a soldier is birthed with one direct order to carry out: "Keep the new decision alive and well."

Now, fast-forward to the present. You decide you want to enhance your ability to relate to the significant others in your life. You want to express yourself meaningfully.

You want to really hear and understand who that other person is and what is important to them. The 'express yourself' soldier is birthed. The 'listen and understand others' soldier packs his bags and marches out into your world.

Just a bit down the road these two new soldiers meet up with a couple of old-timers. The 'keep your important thoughts and feelings to yourself' soldier, who is highly decorated for exceptional performance in the line of duty, and the 'even if confused make believe you understand' soldier, who was promoted to lieutenant colonel years ago, are standing at attention in the middle of the road.

The two new soldiers are fired up and ready to fight. The two seasoned soldiers are skilled in warfare and have been on active duty for a long time. The battle begins.

Meanwhile, you are feeling emotionally exhausted and unable to move forward. One minute you are expressing your thoughts and feelings. The next moment you are making believe you understand when you really don't. The old decision 'don't care deeply' joins the fray and suddenly you want to withdraw and hide from everyone.

Instead of giving up, maybe it is time to call back the troops. **When past decisions collide with your present intentions, doubt, fear, and confusion begin to set in.**

1. When internal battles rage, ask for guidance to discover and uncover old beliefs that no longer serve you.

2. Take your energy and power back by recognizing that when you seem to be stopped and confused it may be due to the result of your operating at cross purposes; two beliefs fighting against each other.

3. Call a ceasefire. Instead of being afraid of your energy and labeling yourself confused and depressed, realize how well your soldiers have fought for your past beliefs and call them home. Thank your soldiers for their commitment and service to past decisions and give them an honorable discharge. Then give them and yourself some R and R.

Notice that inner peace can be restored only through self-patience. Take some quiet time to gain clarity on your present intentions and whether they line up with your deepest needs, values, and goals of today. This is a good time to check in and make sure that your I Am and I Am Letting Go statements are still valid. If they need to be altered, take time to do that now.

> *Decide to treat yourself and your ever-evolving life process with kindness. Send your soldiers on a mission of peace—peace of mind.*

The War is Over

Imagine that you stop at your mailbox today and there, tucked between the junk mail and the bills, is a handwritten, hand-stamped envelope addressed to you.

When you open it, there is a letter inside that says: "This is to inform you that the Universe is friendly, and is particularly fond of and friendly to you." Warmest Regards, The Powers That Be.

What if you believed that message? How would your personal experience of your life change? What struggles and problems would you let go of as you realized they are not as real as you thought, that they are actually more creations of an overactive and critical mind?

How many chronic worries could you allow to fade into the background because you could finally relax your over-vigilant viewing of your life's situations and let up on looking for problematic elements just waiting to find you?

Now, you might be feeling a bit resistant to the notion that you have been living like a paranoid personality, thinking everyone is out to get you.

Actually, I am sure that is not really the case. As a matter of fact, you are probably at a stage in your development where you really believe that life is no longer out to get you. You are unwilling to be victimized.

You are probably quite able to identify yourself as and give yourself credit for being very responsible about the creation of a life that works for you. It is a good bet that you have weathered many storms that have made you strong. Therefore, you are clearly a survivor.

This is all good and necessary to the development of your personal power and authority.

> *Now it is time to move past surviving and into thriving. Thriving requires a whole new set of skills.*

You actually started life with the exact qualities necessary for thriving. They simply went underground as you interacted more with the world and started to amass unpleasant life experiences that led you to decide, perhaps unconsciously and as a felt-sense, that the Universe is often unfriendly and, more important, it seems particularly unfriendly to you.

When a child is safe, secure, and loved, he or she is filled with boundless energy, curiosity, wonder, and unbridled exuberance.

> *Thriving comes packaged as a zest for living and contains within it the skills of being in the present and in touch with what we think, feel, and want.*

Even if we have moved past being victimized by life, most of us have not crossed over the sea of propriety and moved on to the shore of exuberant, passionate, positive regard for ourselves and our lives.

Instead, we stay safely anchored to our habitual, predictable, logical, polite, careful, and consistent attitudes and behaviors.

We opt for good instead of great. We lead acceptable, protected, safe, closed, and invisible lives.

The price is loss of exuberance, then passion, then energy, then motivation, then interest until we become bored and boring energy drains shuffling through tedious days, weeks, months, and years.

We dangerously flirt with either succumbing to a mindless, intentionless existence or we create a life crisis that shakes us to the bone and wakes us up for a minute because our survival is once again threatened.

It is now time to take this message from the Universe to heart. "The Universe is friendly and is particularly fond of and friendly to you." Step up and embrace the position of a favored and loved child of the Universe. Give yourself permission to remove the garb of a foot soldier trudging through dangerous and rocky terrain.

Step out into the light of a grassy summer meadow filled with warm and friendly air and a clear blue sky. Breathe deeply into the endless variety of your life's mood, rhythm, timing, and tempo and allow yourself the freedom to set the clear intention to thrive instead of merely survive.

⌒ *Send a response back to the Universe saying:*
"Thank you for your love and support. I am
ready and willing to allow you to surprise and
delight me now."

Intend. Allow. And remember you are safe enough to relax and receive. The internal war is over.

Hostage Hall

Imagine with me that you are standing with your legs firmly planted on a wide and solid path. You are facing forward. Take a moment to notice as much as you can around you. Take note of what your path looks like. Look to the left and to the right and notice the expressions of nature that surround you. Pause for as long as you need to and allow yourself to get a felt-sense of this special path.

As you feel into your connection with this path, notice also how you are feeling about the prospect of moving forward. What is your energy level? Take a deep breath and relax into your body. Let it tell you what it is feeling.

Is there a part of you that wants to shrink back and turn your attention away from any thoughts of what the future holds for you? These feelings of hesitation and heaviness are not unusual. Often they indicate that we are still energetically tied to situations from our past that didn't turn out the way we wanted them to.

Now that you have found your path, I want you to take a moment to turn around and look backwards for a moment.

Just behind you and not too far away, you will see a large stone building sitting squarely on your path. This building has bars on the windows and a thick padlocked door with a sign over it that says: Hostage Hall.

This is actually a jail of your own making that you have been unconsciously dragging around with you as you struggle to move forward in your life.

This jail contains everyone that you believe has hurt you, harmed you, and held you back from your true happiness.

As you approach your hostage hall, you will notice there is a wooden bench just to the right of the locked door. Take a moment to sit down on it.

You have an important decision to make at this time. Are you willing to open the door with the large iron key that is dangling from the hook near you, and let your hostages free?

It will require that you no longer use them as your excuse and justification for your lack of full participation in and unhappiness with your life.

When they are freed, you are also free. You are free to take ownership and responsibility for creating a quality life that uniquely suits you. If you are willing to take on this challenge, I want to give you some specific directions on how you can approach it. It would be helpful to have paper and pen available so that you can write down what you experience.

When you open the door, have each person leave one by one. Allow the first person to appear on the threshold, notice who it is, look them in the eye, and say to them: "I forgive you and release you because I want my power back." See what their reaction is. Continue with each person that shows up until your hostage hall is empty. Take as much time as you need to complete this part of the exercise. There might even be some surprises that you didn't expect. Approach the experience with as much curiosity as you can allow.

Is it possible to release everyone once and for all? Probably not. What if you don't want to, or can't, forgive them? Try a second strategy. Look them in the eye and say: "Get out, because I am taking my power back."

The point of this exercise is simply that when we tie our energy up resenting, blaming, and hating people and events from our past, we are too burdened to move forward.

Too much unresolved resentment makes life a struggle and clouds our vision with cynicism and deadening attachment to old, worn-out horror stories. Let go as much as you can. Reground and center your feet on your path. Gently turn your eyes toward new horizons. **Open up, accept, embrace, and take ownership of your considerable personal power.**

Leave your hostage hall in the dust and with a newfound lightness; allow your future to unfold with grace and ease.

⌒ *Remember that the best is yet to come.*

When major life transitions visit us, those are the times when we can feel like *we* are walking a tightrope with no net. Fear, apprehension, worry, and self-doubt are natural companions when life as we have known it takes a sharp left turn.

A change in career, getting married or divorced, starting or ending a relationship, loss through death, kids leaving for college, unexpected troubles or illness—all transpire to test our core mettle.

The benefit of surviving a lifequake is that it gives us an opportunity to assess where we are standing and evaluate what steps need to be taken to allow us to birth new life directions from that which has died.

The great work of starting over is to learn to understand what around us, about us, and within us must be nurtured and enlivened and what must be released and let go.

The task of building anew takes energy. It takes all the personal power we can amass. The funding of core personal identity and power often starts with a wake-up call from a life that is perhaps stuck in some variation of: "Well, I don't feel bad but I don't feel good either."

This state of feeling that we are in limbo can only last for so long. Then it is time to venture out and walk new paths.

If life has dented, bent, hurt, and scarred you but still you find that your instincts tell you that this is an opportunity to wizen rather than whither, connect to your unique inner path once again and begin to move forward from here.

CHAPTER 5   SPARKING NEW POSSIBILITIES

Imagine that you decide to take on the task of rearranging your dresser drawers. Each drawer is brimming with clothes that you currently wear, some that no longer fit, and some that were pushed into the bottom drawers quite some time ago and to which you haven't given a moment's glance since.

If you could simply empty each drawer and take time to decide what to do with each item, the task would be manageable.

What if you were restricted from completely emptying the drawers; instead you are required to open each drawer, put both hands in and try to decide what to keep, what to discard, and how to organize everything without completely starting over?

When we begin to examine our lives, we are faced with new decisions about what we want to foster, what we want to discard, and what aspects of our lives we cherish and want to continue to nurture.

Re-arranging our lives can seem daunting. The challenge is made more complex because we already have an active, involved life that was birthed from decisions we made when our wants, needs, and desires were partially out of sight or out of mind.

Our creativity is activated when we open our minds and our hearts to the unformed thoughts, feelings, stirrings, and imaginings that begin to gather at the edges of our awareness, until they can disclose themselves as a burst of light, directing our attention to what we will create next.

Creativity requires room to breathe. Possibility is the womb that enfolds infant desires until they are fully formed enough to be birthed into the harsh light of reality. Creativity is the dark space between the stars.

> *Creativity has quite a few phases and each phase is important to the process. If any part gets interrupted or left out, our new creation is in jeopardy of being scattered to the four winds. Creativity can take the form of a new idea, a new project, or a new vision of what we want to actualize in our lives.*

Whether our creations are tangible or intangible, the steps are the same. Creativity manifests through the interaction of inspiration, concentrated intention, attention to the organization of the steps to be taken, implementation of those steps, and, last but not least, sustenance.

Sustenance is generated when we have given ourselves clear inner permission to create. A solid inner support system is a vital component that provides a core platform that allows us to create at will.

Here is where the partnership between our intuition and our intellect comes in. When the intellect dominates, it glosses over the importance of inspiration, clear intention, and sustenance and simply wants to 'cut to the chase' by mapping out the action steps and implementing them as quickly as possible.

Without a solid connection with our intuition, the still, small voice of inspiration is drowned out. When intellect runs the whole show, it squeezes the life out of our intuitive inspirations. It turns too harsh a light on our budding ideas and it all happens internally.

You say to yourself, "Well, I think I'll create this." The harsh taskmaster inside says, "That's a stupid idea. You have never been able to do anything like that before. Do you know how much effort that will take?

You don't have what it takes. This is another one of your silly ideas. Another wishful-thinking pipe dream." And another idea is stillborn.

To create is **creare** in Latin, meaning to produce, to make life where there was nothing before. When our inner source of inspiration, intuition, is valued, accepted, and respected by our intellect, a loving, caring partnership is formed. When no partnership exists, any effort at a creative act touches off an attack.

We get heavy-handed in the organization and implementation area. We value and concentrate only on the doing of it and ignore the heart of the project.

We short-change our lives and ourselves by over-relying on our ability to make things happen, while discounting the role that incubation in a fertile soil of inner nourishment and support plays in the process of creation.

There is alchemy at work in new growth.

A discontent, fragmented, discordant, demanding, judgmental mind is too infertile and hostile to the light, bright spark of newborn creations.

Creativity requires quiet time to hear the whisperings of our intuitive guidance that will come to us only when our internal climate of swirling random thoughts and feelings is stilled.

We are all blessed with the gift of ownership of our thoughts and feelings. It is our birthright. Few of us have been taught how to be successful stewards of this gift.

Here is how to reverse a negative flow and open to your innate creativity.

- **Decide to take back your creative power.** Recall a time when you were satisfied with something you created. Recapture that feeling and bring it into the present.

- **Respond.** Nurturing your ability to respond to all that goes on around you fuels your creativity. When you exercise the skill of self-expression, it allows you to filter through all of the many possibilities of thought, feeling, action, and reaction. Practice by standing up with and for your own unique responses.

Loss of creativity comes from limiting your choices and suppressing or censoring your deeper feelings and thoughts, or by not saying, doing, or taking action when it would be in your highest and best interests.

- **Let loose.** To create, you must be willing to make room and allow. Give freedom to your ideas, your imagination, and your feelings. Break the habit of criticizing and berating yourself.

- **Protect your time.** Make spaces in your schedule so that you can muse, dream, and imagine a fuller and richer, more rewarding, life.

- **Begin.** If you are scared, begin anyway. If you fail, begin again. If you are mad, sad, frustrated, or fill in the blank, so what. Take another step.

- **Stay with it.** Whether you feel strong or not, ready or not, inspired or not, just keep going, motivated by choice, not by beating yourself about the head and shoulders.

Motivate yourself by continuing to choose those actions that nurture your spirit, your dreams, desires, and plans for wholeness. Allow your motivation to spring from your choosing to love your creative life more than you love cooperating with the habit of abusing and oppressing your personal majesty, soul, passion, and happiness.

The birthright of your soul is rightful authority to fashion your own unique quality of life through the right use of your creative energy.

Nourish, nurture, and value your inner life and you will find the blossoming of your heartfelt creations that will transform your outer experience into the fullness and richness of a wholehearted, positive, passionate life.

Stuck in Emotional and Mental Vertigo

I had a conversation with a woman the other day while sitting at a restaurant counter having lunch.

She was widowed five years ago, had a wonderful marriage, and is presently dating someone who wants to marry her. She is a physically beautiful woman, probably mid-sixties in age, and lived a full, rich, rewarding life with her husband.

She has never worked outside her home and her choices seem to be to either marry someone she likes but is not really passionate about and be financially supported or to get a job, doing who knows what, for minimum wage.

It is obvious that she is highly competent simply by the way she dresses and speaks, and organizes her thoughts and delivers them.

She spent most of her life using her considerable talents and abilities supporting the success of her husband and children. She does not see herself as competent.

She is in emotional and mental vertigo.

The floor dropped out of her life and there does not seem to be anywhere to stand that gives her a bright view of the future.

> I went to the movies yesterday with a friend. We stopped for a cup of coffee after the show and again sat at a counter. There was a woman sitting alone and we started a conversation.
>
> She has been married for thirty-five years; her last child just left for college and her husband left too. She is angry with herself because she has not been able to move herself to take the steps to get a divorce. She is lonely and feels abandoned.
>
> She is caught between wishing her husband would leave his girlfriend and come back so they can live out a fantasy future together and rattling around in an empty house that used to be a home, wondering how in the world she can start over again.

She is in emotional and mental vertigo.

She does not know which way is up and is, therefore, frozen and unable to move because, so far, her options seem dreary.

> I watched a movie the other evening. The story was about a man whose entire career had been in the automotive industry. He was proud of his work and was good at it.
>
> Automation became the innovative way to manufacture cars and the plant at which he was an executive closed down.
>
> He was out of a job and he was over-qualified for the jobs that were available. He was considered too old for management. Corporations were looking for young, bright-eyed men who could be groomed according to the climate of the corporation.
>
> The displaced man got sullen. He got drunk. He got angry. He took it out on his wife and his kids. He lashed out at everyone.

You could feel his pain. He was devastated since his whole career, his life's work, had crumbled before him and disappeared. His anger made perfect sense. He felt important and then he felt worthless. He got mad.

He was in emotional and mental vertigo.

When life as we've known it packs up and leaves, it is devastating, heartbreaking, and terrorizing. When the Vietnam war veterans came home, they were traumatized twice because of lack of validation, support, understanding, or anyone's caring about what they went through.

Surviving the trauma of divorce, the death of your partner, or the loss of a career, like surviving war, takes time. Healing time, sorting time, time to tell your story until you are sick of hearing it.

If you are suffering from a major loss of a marriage, a loved one, or a career, give yourself the gift of generous, extravagant patience.

Going to Nothing

When we have a career that we enjoy, it is most often because we are well suited to it. We find it fulfilling to engage ourselves in whatever pursuit is most fitting to our talents and abilities. What comes along with the ability to perform well is the sense of being in the right place and the right life, and having a special place carved out that has our name on it.

Seeing ourselves as important, unique, and special is an attitude that fosters high self-esteem. Those same beliefs can also contribute to an inflated ego.

When our ego is working overtime, we find ourselves entertaining thoughts that range from "I have so much to do and only I can handle this" to thinking that we are indispensable and must be hypervigilant or our lives will crumble around us in an unsalvageable mess.

Once this kind of thinking takes hold we become ruled by a runaway reactive mind that continuously scans the horizon looking for ways to protect us from any ego-deflating experiences that will knock us off an internal pedestal of being a legend in our own minds.

Ego is a hopeless exaggerator. We will never be as good as our ego thinks we are, nor will we be as bad as the ego thinks, either.

It is a heady experience to successfully juggle myriad roles and responsibilities. Adding more and more plates to spin can be thrilling until the time comes when one too many is added and the whole show starts to come crashing down.

Overload shows up in many different disguises. Sickness is one handy way to make us stop and take a breath. Forgetting important details is another way it shows up. Missing appointments, over-eating, over-drinking, and over-anything is also symptomatic.

One-dimensional thinking and the 'life is hard and then you die' approach is another way to keep going no matter what. The symptoms of overload show up as numbed-out feelings that reduce every day and every experience down to good and bad with no variation of expression.

The antidote to trauma or burnout is to consciously choose to step off the treadmill and go to nothing. Stop physically, mentally, or emotionally overworking.

Turn off the phone, cell phone, computer. Remove yourself from the scene of the crime. Rest your mind. Listen to and hear your emotions. Nurture your physical body. Let go of your hypervigilence. Begin to let yourself down easily and gently.

When we are habitually operating in over-drive, abruptly stopping may create some interesting experiences.

You may discover 'fractured feelings' of happiness, sadness, anxiety, insecurity, fear, apprehension, and plain confusion vying for your attention.

Relaxation may start to visit and then you will be unceremoniously jerked into looking for a solution to a faraway problem that your mind has just conjured up to get you back on the over-thinking treadmill.

> *One of the benefits of going to nothing is that you get an opportunity to come home to yourself.*

Coming home means revisiting what you are doing with your life and whether it is satisfying to you.

Stepping out of the day-to-day routines allows you time to review, overview, and muse about what you like and don't like about the life you are living.

> *Going to nothing is a vote of trust and confidence in the miraculous ability we all possess to create our lives by being willing to choose and choose again.*

As our awareness grows and we give ourselves permission to thrive rather than merely survive, we can be somebody and nobody, give and receive, grab on and let go, take control and surrender.

When we are stuck using all of our energy to fight or flee the perils of day-to-day living, it is time to choose a new path.

This path opens to us when we set a clear intention to thrive. Thriving can be accomplished only through the active courting of grace and ease. Thriving has nothing to do with the circumstances of our lives.

> *Thriving is determined by how much we can ride the winds of change without over-analyzing or over-dramatizing the part we play in the bigger scheme of things.*

Thriving requires a full partnership with all that is well in us and around us. It requires us to accept our basic goodness. It calls for a letting go of obsessing over what is wrong while hoping that things will right themselves magically.

Thriving requires that we give up the struggle, the striving, and the demanding and commanding voices of our unfulfilled dreams in favor of allowing Divine Guidance entrance into our plans.

As we learn to listen to our intuitive voice and seek inspiration and sustenance from within, we can allow ourselves to relax into the knowledge that we need to take only one step at a time to respond well to our lives. Once again, this is where our I Am and I Am Letting Go statements provide a one-pointed inspirational focus.

We can practice walking with a confident stride using both our intuition and our intellect to move gracefully forward, rejuvenated, refreshed, and in step with our own unique rhythm, timing, and tempo.

Then one day, slowly, softly, gently, the healing hands of time will begin to turn you right side up, center your feet back on the ground and, with your Higher Self to guide you, a new chapter of your personal journey will begin to usher you step-by-step back into life.

A Visit to the Cottage in the Woods

Let's take a moment to take a short mental and emotional vacation. The good news about this kind of travel is that there is no commute, no hassles with crowds, and no financial burden before, during, or after the trip.

I want you to simply use your breathing as a way to begin to settle yourself down and trigger your relaxation response.

Feel yourself beginning to let go and relax by breathing rhythmically and gently. There is no need to change the cadence of your breathing. Just breathe in now, and then out, in and out. Pause here as you take time to gently breathe and continue to let down, let go, and relax. Simply tell your body that it is allowed to just go soft.

I want you to imagine that you are standing at the edge of a lush, green forest. This forest is thick with ancient trees. Trees as old as time. And you are beginning to look around until you find a footpath, an entrance way into the woods.

Now begin to look around and explore; do that now. You may have to push some of the overgrown ferns, wildflowers, and full green plants out of the way so that you can begin your journey into the woods.

Once you have placed your feet firmly on the path, begin to follow it. You will notice that this path has a very special feeling about it. There is something very mystical and magical about your surroundings and yet at the same time, though curious, you feel very safe and secure.

You feel a strong sense of protection as though the trees surrounding you are like wise and loving grandparents who look lovingly down on their favorite grandchild. And so as you continue on your journey, you know that you are safe and protected and secure. Pause here for a moment more, to really connect with your sense of safety and security.

As you continue on, you notice, just ahead and up over a small hill, the faint outline of a thatched roof. And as you progress up the hill, you find yourself looking down at a quaint, old-fashioned English cottage nestled among the trees, in a lush, wooded valley.

This cottage is sending out a strong message of welcome and comfort and hospitality, so you begin to quicken your pace and make your way up to the front door.

You reach out and gently turn the doorknob and the door instantly and easily opens up to you. As you enter the cottage, you notice a warm and welcoming fire already lit in the fireplace and a colorful, old-fashioned hand-braided rug on the floor in front of it.

There is an empty rocking chair that beckons you to come and sit and rock for a bit, dreamily watching the flames of the fire dance before your eyes.

And as you sit and restfully rock back and forth, with nothing to do and nowhere to be, you seem to actually begin to float and dream and deeply relax as you gaze into the fire.

And with each rocking motion, you find that your sense of well-being is increasing as you rock away your fears and worries and heartaches and apprehensions.

Simply allow yourself to be cradled in the arms of this comforting rocker, in this magical cottage, so that your innocence can be restored with each rocking motion and your overburdened shoulders can release the cares and concerns you've been shouldering.

Let the cottage restore to you your sense of basic goodness and the basic goodness of your life.

And again, there is nothing for you to do other than give yourself permission to be open and receptive to being restored to a deep and lasting sense of well-being. This sense of well-being that is necessary for you to contact and unite with is yours to have as a gift from this magical cottage in the woods.

Now that you have created this cottage, you can return to it any time you feel you need comforting. It will open its doors to you for the purpose of returning you to your rightful sense of well-being and innocence.

Know that you have created this opportunity for yourself as a validation of your willingness to intentionally open to the restorative powers of being willing to simply go to nothing.

Your Personal Energy Audit

Each of us has a bank of personal energy we can call upon in the pursuit of what we want. Sometimes that bank is rich and full. Other times it becomes depleted.

1. The first account covers the vital area of soulfulness. Your soulfulness account gives you the energy to seek out new knowledge in both your business and personal life that excites you, stimulates you, and inspires you to create and invent new approaches to old situations.

If your soulfulness account is too low or overdrawn it is because you have too many demands on your current resources without having enough replacement energy in the form of receptive time to acknowledge and own your current accomplishments.

You may be using too much of your soulfulness pursuing what you think you should do or have to do rather than what you really care about so that you consistently short-change yourself and end up feeling brittle instead of protected, full, warm, and richly connected to your basic goodness and creativity.

2. The second account is labeled TOO. This account handles the inflow and outflow of deposits and withdrawals of energy gains and energy drains that move in and out of your daily transactions. Check to see if you are overdrawing this account because your life is TOO, either too negative or too positive. Therefore, you are too intensely flowing your energy out until you are worn down through too much account activity.

You may have lost the ability to balance this account because you are under-loved or over-loved, under-worked or over-worked, or faced with too much or too little stimulation.

Too much pull on this account and a fire rages inside. Too little activity and the fire goes out as though it had been drowned with too much water. In the face of too much, you gradually become dry and used up. Your heart gets tired and your energies dissipate and then a mysterious unnamed yearning, a soul hunger, takes over and you begin to feel lost and abandoned.

3. The third account houses those activities and ways of being that are habitual and unconscious. It is an unattended account that yields low interest because it is managed by doing the same things in the same way.

It takes the sparkle from your eyes, makes your bones weary, and keeps you feeling unstimulated and on edge until you no longer have any idea who or what your life is about. You feel starved for affection, for stimulation, for more meaningful engagement in your life. You also find yourself stuck in futile and unyielding relationships and jobs and, ultimately, your life.

This account can be revitalized only when you are willing to give up the erroneous and often unconscious belief that you will get more spiritual credit for being long-suffering or that if you work hard at something that doesn't feed you, you will finally prove you are acceptable and worthy.

4. The fourth vital account is used for the protection of your inner core. This is the place where you store your valuables for safekeeping. This is your safety deposit and is meant to protect your spark of wonder, your vision for your best future, and your peace of mind.

It protects your freedom from worry and your freedom from constant demands and bombardments to your peace of mind from the mundane stresses and strains of life.

To establish a substantial, full, rich, and abundant inner core you must learn to redeem your inner calmness and peace by seeking time to muse and dream, to contemplate, to learn, and to uncover and discover the forgotten, the disowned, and the disused aspects of yourself.

Taking this time will allow you to begin to imagine your future and put to rest the scars of your past so that you can access the inner wisdom that is your true inheritance.

In acknowledgement of your desire to build a substantial spiritual portfolio in these four vital accounts your best future self will meet you in the safety deposit vault. You will be handed a key and together you will each use your keys in the two locks and then slide the metal box out and sit down at the table provided.

Inside the box, you will find a specific symbol of your growing inner wealth and abundance that is a gift and an acknowledgement of your willingness to come home to yourself and intentionally make new choices that will allow you to truly thrive.

The symbol will appear to you in the form that is best suited to you. Remember there is nothing for you to do other than to be open and receptive to receiving this gift. This symbol will stay with you as a visionary talisman…connecting you to your growing powers of insight, passion and connection to your inner core and intuitive nature.

Resurrecting New Vision

Before we can fully access our intuitive knowing, we must first awaken to the information available through our five senses.

When our senses are dulled by rigid opinions, old grudges, worn-out habits and stagnant, lifeless ways of seeing, we are overburdening our nervous systems with static. Nothing new emanates from deadened circuits.

To activate the innate gift of intuitive vision, we must see our world with new eyes and hear past the mundane into the heart of issues. We must be willing to taste life fully and be touched by our experiences.

I can hear you now: "Isn't there the no-cost, no-frills, basic icing on-the-cake, all-benefit and no-price plan? Can't I get intuitive powers and secret, special information that I can add to everything else I already know so that I can be safe, right, and perfect?"

In a word, no. Intuition synthesizes all the information gleaned from our five senses. If our basic instincts are shut down, rigidly calcified and numb, then we have no open channel to access our intuitive knowing. We are stuck with poor reception.

It is like having the cable disconnected on your TV. The information is there but you've lost access to it. So…what to do?

A first step is to begin to approach the issues in your life in a new way. Rather than asking yourself "What should I do?" and then over-thinking and over-analyzing, ask, "How many ways can I view this situation to open to new information?"

If you are willing to give this a try, I am going to give you a step-by-step way to do this. First you will need some quiet time and the willingness to step out of the game for a half an hour or so. Bring pen and paper.

1. Write down the issue, problem, or situation that is currently causing you confusion as succinctly as you can. "The problem I am facing is…" Once you have homed in on the clearest statement you can make, you are ready for the next step.

2. Write down everything that you presently know about this issue as fast as you can. Hold nothing back. Simply allow the information to tumble out from your pen. Disregard the order. Allow the information to pour out in whatever order it chooses. Feelings. Heart hurts, embarrassments, wonderings, concerns, imaginings, knowns, unknowns, figments of your imagination. Critical judgments. Fears. Apprehensions. Worst-case scenarios. Access all information presently available to you until nothing else comes to mind.

Now let's play with ways to open to new information.

3. If this issue had a smell, what would it smell like? Write that down.

4. If it had a taste, what would it taste like?

5. If you had a truth serum that all parties could take, what would the real truth about this situation be?

6. If you could see beyond the surface reality of the situation, what would you see?

7. If you touched the issue and allowed the issue to touch you deeply, what would your true, touching feelings be?

8. If you could hear beyond the surface words into the heart of the matter, what deeper messages would be lurking there?

9. If you had a magnifying glass, what would be coming clear to you now? Now let's go one step further.

10. If the situation were an animal, what kind of animal would it be? What are the characteristics of this animal? Write that down.

11. If you were an animal, what would you be and what would your predominant characteristics be? Are there any others involved? If so, decide what animal each person is and their characteristics.

The writing part is now finished.

Next, let's check in on your attitude. Are you willing to really listen and hear the truth of the matter? Can you give yourself permission to trust yourself to do what is life-giving and enhancing rather than look outside yourself for answers? Will you allow yourself to 'not know what to do' until you can see with a clearer vision and take the actions that spring from there?

The last step is to mentally and emotionally let go of the situation for a while and be patient. The new energies are now activated. Your intuition is engaged.

One of two things will happen. You will immediately get new insights and clarity about the situation along with the right actions to take or you still will not know what to do.

If you are still unclear, don't panic. Your next step is to do nothing. Push the pause button. Hold. Allow things to play out. This is where trust comes into play. Trust that clarity and direction will come to you in its own time and in exactly the correct way. Don't take my word for it. Simply try the exercise for yourself.

Intuition is a gift that is available to you as a source of information and inspiration.

Intuitive knowledge comes as a result of taking your life more seriously. Not the serious that means consistent, predictable, rigid, cold, hard, factual, numb, nose to the grindstone.

The serious that goes toe-to-toe with life.

The serious that is willing to put in a heartfelt and intentional request and is also willing to make the necessary adjustments to actualize new visions.

The serious that is willing to let go of outmoded ways of being to muster up the courage to stand up, fully participate, and respond to life with all systems on Go.

Decide to resurrect the serious that allows you to begin to take the steps necessary to activate true joy and pleasure as you master the art of living fully engaged.

Relaxing Into Wholeness

When we are intent on really feeling good about our lives and ourselves, it takes a level of personal mastery to allow thriving to be our predominant experience. Positive thinking is one aspect of living well. Positive feeling is another.

Positive thoughts married to positive feelings and living in the same body at the same time can seem as random, elusive, and mysterious as the phenomenon of spontaneous healings or unexplainable miracles, given the fast-paced, unpredictable world we live in.

We are each a mass of moment-to-moment thoughts and feelings that randomly collide and, if given free rein, will determine whether we have a good day or a bad day.

> *If we truly want to create a life that is grounded in basic well-being, we must decide to commit ourselves to learning what it takes to thrive instead of merely survive.*

As I see it, there are two well-traveled roads that make up our usual approach to dealing with our lives. We habitually allow life to overpower us and, as a result, we find ourselves living in the land of passive victimhood.

When we get tired of the short end of the stick, we rally all our reserves and fight the good fight. No matter what life throws at us, we never surrender. We are on automatic pilot, constantly striving and lusting after something that is out of our reach.

Though this seems like the courageous, strong, powerful, and preferred approach to living successfully, on closer inspection, we are simply trading in passive victimhood to become a card-carrying, full-time member of the active victim club.

At least active victims bring a dramatic flair to their tales of insurmountable odds and of how they triumphed or suffered temporary defeat. Active victimhood is much more entertaining and energizing than being the downtrodden underdog who has fallen down and can't get up.

Limited understanding and lack of expanded vision conspire to create the common experience of using either/or, good/bad, right/wrong, better than/less than thinking to maintain our preferred stance of either passive victim or active victim.

Walking Our Talk

In order to be secure enough to own both our wins and losses, we must first invest the time and the energy necessary to discover the core needs and values that drive our lives.

As children we usually adopt the attitudes and beliefs of our family of origin. When those learned values go unquestioned, our lives become driven by external forces. Our inherited family values may be solid and worthy but it is still necessary to personally examine and then directly either choose them as our own or reject them, depending on our unique needs, desires, and goals.

For example, perhaps you were brought up in a family that values intellectual pursuits to the exclusion of feelings, affiliations, and relationships. Achievement focus reigns supreme.

Suppose you have a strong leaning toward amiability and establishing loyal connections with others. Your natural style is relationship oriented and you have an innate personality style that is easygoing, supportive, and non-competitive.

A conflict can arise between your need for closeness and connection with others and your family's top value of mental challenges, accomplishment, and achievement.

Left unexplored and swallowed whole, you could spend the rest of your life feeling less than and inadequate because you don't measure up to the standards of your learned programming. The incompatibility between your need for strong connections and your learned value of high achievement could leave your thoughts and feelings in serious conflict.

If you strive for accomplishment and become competitive with others, you will think your actions are good but you will feel bad. If you maintain accepting, easy relationships and give up high achievement to be more cooperative and amiable, you will feel good but think your non-competitive stance is bad.

Walking our talk requires that we intentionally decide to discover our unique way of seeing the world and consciously choose to establish values that are congruent with our needs and desires. When we carry out the commitment to discover our core values, our thoughts and feelings can begin to work in tandem.

Conflict and confusion between our thoughts and feelings ends because we actively begin to take responsibility for meeting our own needs.

We choose values to live by and a code of ethics from which we can direct our lives. With our core values clearly defined, we can identify those pursuits that will give our lives direction and meaning.

We will be able to envision a life purpose that is guided by values that are current and alive with personal meaning rather than being stagnant and inherited from someone else's passionate pursuits.

When we are adrift without a purpose that lifts us above our insecurities, all we are left with is our moment-to-moment thoughts and feelings. Giving over our lives to the endless clamoring of our inner critic and over-active imaginations is a formula for a crazy, confused life.

When we make the decision to walk our talk, to live our lives from the essence of who we are, we must be willing to pay at least three up-front prices.

1. We must be willing to be visible.
2. We must be willing to be vulnerable. We must be willing to take new risks—appropriate risks, not crazy risks.
3. We must be willing to open up to ourselves, to life and to guidance from our spiritual source.

Open up and listen to your answers to some deeper questions:

What is missing in my life? What do I stand for? What do I truly value? How do I know that? Does my behavior reflect my core values? What am I really about? Do I have principles that I honor with my behavior? What do my actions say about me? How do I treat myself? How do I treat others? Am I trustworthy? Do I trust myself? If not, why not?

When we take the time to delve under the surface of our habitual lives, we begin the process of hunting for the treasures and wisdom that come from the examined life.

Then we can create a strong foundation of self-knowledge built from a blending of our unique needs, desires, dreams, and values so that we truly walk our talk.

The Rowboat of Life

In order to take responsibility for our lives, we must foster a fully functioning relationship with our personal power. A strong physical body, mental body, emotional body, and spiritual body all functioning together is the essence of personal power. The trickiest part of this equation is getting our intellect and emotions to cooperate with each other.

Imagine with me that these two energy sources are sitting in a rowboat in the middle of a lake. Each is in charge of an oar.

Intellect sits on the right and is tall and lean with long arms and legs. He is focused, methodical, and systematic in his approach to rowing.

He is focused on the goal of getting to the shore and has decided that strong, shallow strokes repeated with the same intensity will get to the goal the fastest.

Emotion is sitting to his left. She is short, full-figured, and spontaneous. She loves the look of the sun on the water. She savors the experience of the rocking boat, the soothing sounds of nature, and the gentle kisses of the fresh, fragrant air.

She is in no hurry. There is so much to see. She is enjoying the feel of the smooth wooden oar. She leans over her side of the boat and tries to touch the bottom of the lake with her oar to find its depth.

Intellect begins to row. He methodically counts the strokes as he tries to move forward.

Emotion is still holding her oar deeply in the water, while Intellect consistently tries to move ahead.

The boat spins dizzily to the left. She laughs. He frowns. He stops rowing in exasperation.

She begins to row by herself. The boat glides around in circles to the right, sending ripples out on the lake but making no progress other than drifting and spinning in place.

He tells her to stop causing trouble. There is a right way and a wrong way to row. He is right. She is wrong.

She turns her back on him and lifts her face to the sun. She refuses to participate and amuses herself by trailing her hand in the water.

He wishes he could push her overboard. He wants to grab her oar and do the whole job himself. Time is being wasted. He is getting nowhere fast.

He is stuck. He is going to have to make peace with her or they will never get anywhere.

He swallows hard and tries to apologize for his rude behavior.

She says he doesn't sound sincere. That is because he isn't. He doesn't really want to deal with her. He just wants to get the job done.

She tells him that she will cooperate only if he chills out and stops ruining her trip with his obsessive striving.

She points out that it is a beautiful day and that she wants to enjoy the process of the trip instead of just getting to shore as quickly as possible. She mentions the beauty of the colors in the water and how peaceful it is on this lake.

He does have to admit that the trip would be more enjoyable if he could relax a bit. Relaxation has never been his strong suit. He apologizes again, more sincerely this time. She smiles and accepts his gesture of friendship.

She concedes that shallower strokes would probably work better but also points out that her arms are not as long as his so her natural, more comfortable stroke will still be deeper and less far-reaching than his.

He agrees to slow down his pace. She shallows up her stroke and increases her rhythm. They begin to move forward. Sitting next to each other, they find a cadence. He has given a little and so has she.

He takes a deep breath of fresh air and realizes that he is almost enjoying himself. He still has his eye on the shore but he is also allowing some pleasure to filter through. Insight surfaces that this seems easier than his normal striving stance. He can feel his muscles rippling, relaxing, and tensing as the boat moves forward easily and effortlessly.

Emotion becomes enamored with the quickly passing scenery. It seems like a mosaic; a kaleidoscope of colors, shapes, smells, and feelings. She delights in the forward movement.

Her senses are alive and vibrant. She feels energized and accomplished at the same time. She is still not concerned with the destination but notices a certain thrill that comes from the fact that progress is being made.

Intellect is satisfied with their results. He wants to say *his* results but in all fairness, he acknowledges that she is doing her part and it is easier and more enjoyable to work together.

Emotion is becoming fonder of him and their newly established partnership. She is hopeful that they will continue to grow in their respect for each other.

This story is about the masculine and feminine energy in all of us. Our intellects like to try to control everything. It seems faster and more efficient that way. Feelings are inconsistent and uncontrollable. But our job is to create a working partnership between our thoughts and our feelings.

For a partnership to emerge, we need to slow our intellect down to make room for experiences. It won't work to turn all the power over to our feelings because we will forfeit our ability to manifest results. When each aspect is treated with respect, life becomes easier. We can move forward enjoyably instead of just rapidly.

Once the partnership begins to work, watch out that your intellect doesn't try to take all the credit or try to re-establish itself as the top dog.

Your feeling nature longs to be included and is endlessly cooperative as long as her participation is respected and accepted. If she is taken for granted, you are asking for trouble. She will sabotage your plans by turning her back and withdrawing her exuberance.

She will hide her participation under a heavy cloak of resistance, resentment, and revenge, leaving your life bogged down in a cloud of anxiety and depression.

When this partnership is nurtured and held respectfully, life truly begins to flow. Easily, rhythmically, gently, enjoyably...one stroke after another.

A Power Play

It was around seven in the evening one holiday and all of my grandchildren were keeping themselves busy in different rooms of the house.

Elena, who was seven, and her cousin Jake, who was six, were playing together in the living room. I sat down on the couch to listen in. They were deeply engaged in a made-up game called King and Slave.

Elena, sitting on the big chair said in a commanding voice: "Slave, get me that stool." Jake followed her pointing finger and reluctantly carried the small embroidered stool over and placed it in front of her. "Now, move it back" she said. Jake sighed and did as he was told. "Now turn on the light," ordered the king. Jake threw up his hands and said to the air: "This is the worst game I've ever played!"

Elena didn't even blink. She just said: "Okay, now *you* can be the king." Jake's body immediately relaxed in a "Now this is more like it" kind of response. He then planted himself firmly on the throne that Elena had just vacated.

"Slave, would you please bring me that stool?" Jake said, with his polite manners training showing. "The king doesn't have to say please or thank you," said Elena as she disdainfully got the stool and carelessly put it down in front of him.

I guess I must have let out a little laugh because the king turned his attention toward me and then back to the slave with a firm command: "Slave, take Grandma California away." This order took Elena by surprise. Inanimate objects presented no problem but the king had just bumped up the stakes. After all, the grandmother might say no and then what? I was very cooperative and left the room without resisting my slave leader.

I also came right back but was allowed to stay because I let them know that I was now a statue of a grandmother, not a real grandmother. Both king and slave easily agreed with my new identity. I guess the most important thing was that they could see that I wasn't being defiant. As a statue, I didn't pose any threat to the king's authority or the slave's authority either.

Shortly, Kyle, who was five and Elena's younger brother, tried to enter the game. Jake gave him an order and then Elena did too but he was too eager to please. They left him turning on and off the light switch with no new orders coming until he said he was bored and left the room.

It was a fascinating glimpse at how authority was perceived as permission to demand and command performance from others. Politeness and hesitation were interpreted as weakness. When in the slave position, personal power was communicated through a negative bend towards carelessness and thinly disguised disdain.

In order for the game to continue, there had to be just enough resistance present between the players. When Kyle brought an undisguised willingness to follow anyone's orders, all players lost interest. No tension, no game.

Better than, less than, dominant, submissive, ruler, ruled, strong, weak, hard, soft, direct, responsive; witnessing their imaginative play was like watching energy dance. They defined their roles and then played at trading places, all with an ease and enthusiasm that allowed their interaction to continue until their interest was spent.

Androgyny is a term used to define the presence of both masculine and feminine characteristics. In fact, masculine and feminine attributes, when freed through spontaneous creativity, perpetually pass into one another. Fluid hardens to solid, solid rushes to fluid.

Watching their play was a perfect example of the fact that there is no wholly masculine, no purely feminine. When rigid definitions of what is masculine and what is feminine are removed, active and receptive energy can move and flow.

By six and seven, both Elena and Jake have ingested the societal dictate that it is better to 'be a hammer than a nail'.

Perhaps our challenge as a society is to elevate kindness, compassion, cooperation, receptivity, and service to others as a necessary and equal partner to power.

When power and service marry, it becomes possible to create interdependent relationships where we can interact with both active and receptive energies engaged.

The number one definition of *king* is a monarch who inherits the position and rules for life. When we surrender the crown, it becomes possible to engage our personal power, our ability to act, influence, inspire, and produce.

When we reject the negative definition of slave as someone who has lost control and is dominated by something or someone, we can cultivate the ability to be directly responsive, response-able, to our own needs as well as being energetic contributors to the welfare of others.

CHAPTER 6   WALKING THROUGH THE DOORS AND COMING HOME

Imagine with me that you are walking down a long, narrow hallway. There are four doors, two doors on the left and two on the right, and they are all closed.

There is a sign on each door.

⁓ One door says SOFTEN.

⁓ The second door says DEEPEN.

⁓ The third: OPEN TO.

⁓ The fourth: STRENGTHEN.

Take a moment to assess which doors most need your attention.

1. The door marked **Soften** asks you to look for those past experiences that may have led you to harden your heart towards life.

Are you presently operating from a belief that life and the people in it are in some way out to get you? Therefore, you must be wary, suspicious, forever on your toes; staying ahead of the game to keep yourself safe.

2. The second door is marked **Deepen.** If this door captures your attention, it may be time for you to begin to expand your self-definition past what is presently comfortable and safe.

What are you withholding from life and what are you giving instead? Are you friendly and accommodating but less engaged, involved, and committed then you could be? Are you skimming the surface of your relationships so that you never make any waves?

Do you secretly hope that something exciting and passion-filled will come and sweep you away instead of being willing to take the risks to create your life with bold *yes* and *no* strokes rather than with 'maybe, sort of, I guess, whatever you say' lukewarm attention?

3. Door number three is marked **Open To**. This door leads to all the unexplored paths that have been ignored or given very little attention.

Perhaps you have been so driven by career success that there has been no time or inclination to develop any other interests.

Do you enjoy music, theatre, sports, literature, and travel, or certain types of people, yet never make any time to pursue or experience the fulfillment of these interests?

Do you only sing one song? Are you defined by your position in life, your position power, and feel out of place and inept without the protection of your roles and established routines?

It may be time to open to new experiences just for the stimulation that newness brings.

4. The last door is marked **Strengthen**. Perhaps this door is beckoning because it is time to invite discipline into your life.

Are you craving more freedom, more permission to do what you want to do when you want to do it?

The pursuit of unlimited freedom is a false journey that leads to the unrealistic expectation that life owes you a comfortable, privileged life. Freedom becomes possible when you have made sure that discipline has an established home with you.

Discipline equals freedom. If this door speaks to you, begin to directly look for those aspects of yourself that need shoring up. Do you have too much clutter in your life, whether physical, mental, or emotional, or all of the above? Have you let too many things slide? Have you started too many projects that are left unfinished?

Do you make commitments to yourself that you never keep? Have you become weak in your own self-knowledge by making excuses for yourself because *that is just the way you are?*

Life is change; growth is optional. When you decide to take on the task of personal growth, though knowledge of ourselves is a difficult study, the rewards are self-respect and self-trust.

Soften

If this door is calling to you, enter and begin the task of softening your hold on trying to control everything and let your mind and heart soften to the task of beginning to regain and build trust with yourself and others by releasing the fear of being taken advantage of and the anger that fuels that belief.

HEART HURTS

Deep down, each of us is vulnerable to feelings of inadequacy and to self-questioning, self-doubt, and self-criticism.

Sitting offside from our daily mundane awareness is the unsettling knowledge that we are capable of being wounded. We know that because we have the inner scars to prove it.

Penetrate deeply into the secret existence of anyone, even of someone that seems particularly happy, and their interior landscape will house pockets of desolation, emptiness, and heart-hurts that have left rough scar tissue and heaps of unclaimed and abandoned rubbish from past traumas, struggles, and disappointments.

The most common antidote used to counteract lurking feelings of inadequacy is overdoing. When every waking moment is spoken for, the gifts that come from inner solitude are withdrawn.

Solitude is the necessary component of self-renewal. Without it, we divorce ourselves from true inward quietness; the soil from which solid self-support and self-knowledge grows.

Here is the paradox. Many highly intelligent, productive, successful people are limping through their lives crippled by heart-squeezing loneliness.

Solitude is one thing. Loneliness is another.

Loneliness is born out of the lack of connection to our deeper needs, wishes, hopes, dreams and desires — those longings that will only whisper/speak when we are quiet and inward — attracted rather than lusting after external outcomes and results.

Solitude is the nurturer of our inner richness but will not feed guests that come to his table empty-handed. **Solitude hosts a banquet, not a soup kitchen.** Solitude will not entertain us when we just give it scraps of ourselves, scraps of our time, and scraps of our thoughts.

When we refuse to respond to the needs of our spirit, we abandon ourselves. The denied self will be patient only for only so long. The muffled cry of our neglected soul work begins to seek out ways of amplifying its voice. Like the irritation of the sand in the oyster's shell, loneliness and the feeling of being unwanted begin to take hold. Nothing satisfies that insistent longing to be connected.

We try to seek out others to fill the void.

Unfortunately, they are usually trying to do the same; therefore, the terrible inner poverty just gets magnified. Neither person wants to risk the terror of opening up to another because of the fear of being criticized, misunderstood, or rejected when they are already heavy-handed with themselves.

Addressing this relationship between loneliness and solitude is challenging and intriguing. If it required following an analytical, step-by-step process, the successful high achiever would have no problem.

Block out some time, pick a compelling place, and sign up for some rest and relaxation.

But it isn't that easy because "no matter where you go, there you are." We cannot grow and progress in a vacuum. We all need a safe place where we can debrief. We need to be able to hear ourselves muse out loud in the company of at least one other awake and aware person. We need to see ourselves mirrored in the accepting eyes of another. Having someone to tell is one of the fundamental needs of human beings.

Self-esteem is cultivated from the marriage of the deep knowledge that we are both capable and lovable. We can endlessly prove our capabilities by stacking up accolades, awards, degrees, and the accoutrements of success.

But the lovable part of the self-esteem equation requires that we take on the messy business of surrendering our armor.

Self-support and self-knowledge are incubated, cultivated, and fed through the process of timidly or boldly involving ourselves in the dance of giving to and receiving from others while continuing to build the inner stability that comes from living a purposeful and productive life.

UNDERSTANDING OTHERS

It is impossible to access true intuitive guidance and direction when we insist on rigidly holding on to our favorite fantasies about how other people should treat us.

When upset visits in the form of an uncomfortable confrontation with another, it is easy to come to the conclusion that it is personal. After all, out of the blue *you* are attacked and invasively confronted with lies and crazy-making accusations. Of course it is personal.

Let's look more closely. If you decide that this person is out to get you and that is the only possible option, your response will be limited to defensive and reactive anger or outrage. They accuse and you explain, justify, and defend your position.

They make you wrong. You disagree. They confront. You retaliate. The battle starts and then accelerates rapidly. The point of view that others are out to get you generates righteous anger, fear, and threatened reactions.

There is another point of view that is not so obvious but if you look closely it is often more accurate. Instead of jumping to the conclusion that 'they are out to get you', what if their behavior simply gives you clear information about who this person is when threatened?

This is their habitual reaction. They are on automatic pilot, perpetually threatened, resistant, resentful, worried, scared, out of control, and reactive, and the result is crazy, nonsensical behavior.

Every upset requires willing participants. Let's say it starts with your saying something offensive to me. I retaliate. The disagreement is solidified at that moment. It is birthed into form. Arguments exist in the space that becomes locked in between you and me. If I take the interaction personally, I take the bait and turn your fantasy into a reality. If, instead, I take *me* out of it, I am free to see your behavior clearly without my interpretation creating a negative meeting of two minds.

If we could penetrate deeply into the secret existence of those around us, we would come upon things they expend a lot of effort to hide.

We all carry bare places, heaps of old rubble that hasn't been cleared away, cold heart spaces, desolate and lonely places that breed fantasies that the world is out to get us and that we are impotent to do anything about it. Impotence breeds fear.

Aggression or submission is the instinctive response to fear. In fear, we forget who we are.

When fearful we are unprepared to approach situations with clarity and sanity. Therefore, it is reasonable to assume that the chances of having a confusing and crazy confrontational interaction with another are high.

Seen in this light, it is a miracle that any enjoyable and satisfying human relations ever exist between people of different standards.

When we let go of the idea that the world is out to get us, we are free to take the appropriate measures to protect ourselves and our peace of mind.

Using some exaggerated examples, let's explore the two points of view. If a rainstorm starts and I take it personally, I will rile at the weather for ruining my plans. I will fantasize that the weather is particularly hostile towards me because every time I decide to plan an outdoor party it rains.

Or let's say I pick up a kitten and it scratches me and I take the kitten's actions personally. I decide that the kitten doesn't like me and scratched me intentionally and maliciously.

If I take the position that rain just does what it does, I can take the proper measures to protect myself. I can check the weather report before I plan an outdoor party. I can wear a raincoat and bring an umbrella if I don't want to get wet.

I can realize that kittens scratch. That is just what they do. Therefore, I can wear long sleeves before picking the kitten up. I can wear gloves or stay far enough away from the kitten so that I don't get scratched.

If you find yourself revisiting an upsetting incident long after the actual event took place, this is an excellent time to stop and do a reality check.

Answer the following question by giving it honest and thoughtful consideration: Do you believe this person is truly out to get you?

If your answer is yes, then what specifically would cause this person to be after you? Check to make sure that your reasons are not simply a fantasy that you made up from your personal grab bag of unfinished business.

If you still come up with a clear yes, they are definitely out to get you, then take the proper defensive measures. Get a lawyer, a restraining order, or a bodyguard, or enter the witness protection program.

If your answer is no, they are not out to get you, then here is the next question: Is this just the way they are?

If you find that your answer shows up as a little bit of both, then you will be able to determine the specific right action for you to take on the part that is about you and let go of the rest.

When you can view this person through a wider lens, then it becomes apparent that the behaviors they are displaying with you are often more habitual than intentional.

Once you are clear, then you are free to make whatever decisions are necessary to protect yourself and your sanity rather than adding your own insecurities to the fray.

> *True self-respect requires that we respect the choices of others and at the same time respect our own ability and right to choose what we will and will not participate in.*

Heart Smarts

We can enlist our heart skills to open and close, extend and receive, lighten, soften, let go and let down, stand up and stand out as exquisite responses to the rhythm, timing, and tempo of our unique life challenges and intrigues.

Strong-hearted, openhearted, warm-hearted, and **light-hearted** are worthy and useful companions on the journey towards living well through right use and ownership of our personal power.

1. Maintaining personal boundaries, knowing what *we* want and being *self*-protective and able to stand up for *our* values helps to create the experience of being well cared for and self-confident. We will call this strong-hearted versus timid or weak-hearted.

2. Sharing personal experiences that give others a glimpse into our private worlds, extending ourselves beyond our comfort zones, letting the light of a new day shine on old, habitual feelings and stagnant thoughts, and exposing ourselves to new interactions and experiences, all serve to

bring new movement and flexibility into our lives. We will name this open-hearted versus closed-hearted.

3. Being willing to take into consideration the feelings, sensibilities, and uniqueness of others and connect with them through the common ground of mutual feelings, extending good will and positive regard, and empathizing with the fact that everyone is doing the best they can with what they have to draw from, allows a sense of overall well-being to permeate our lives. This can be called warm-hearted or soft-hearted versus cold-hearted or hard-hearted.

4. Approaching life situations with a kind and gentle touch, opening up to the quirky humor that sometimes bubbles up, brewed from the mix that is created when what we hope and expect meets with what life actually brings us, and letting go of our tight-fisted attempts to control the game helps to air out and dispel the heavy, overwhelmed, and burdened thoughts and feelings that accumulate from shouldering too much for too long. We will call this light-hearted versus heavy-hearted.

The shift that must be made to access these skills is in our awareness of the role that heart smarts play in the task of living well. Heart skills are usually relegated to second-string status, positioned as the secretary of the intellect.

In this position, our feeling nature simply takes dictation from the boss and carries out the mundane tasks of producing conventional feelings that support the decisions of the intellect-in-charge.

Used this way our heart's intelligence is repressed and therefore manufactures resentment; suppresses grief, sadness, and anger; and stays mute when in disagreement with the intellect.

As a result, we stay stuck in the experience of too much boredom and numbness from holding back our natural feelings of exuberance, creativity, curiosity, and passion. Seen this way, there is a storehouse of energy ready and waiting to be called into service.

Resolve to liberate your heart's intelligence and promote them to executive status. Imagine creating a dream team of strength, openness, warmth, kindness, caring, and delight that can partner with your intuition to co-create a life infused with a sense of well-being and mastery.

Deepen

If the **Deepen** door is the one you choose, enter in and begin the process of exploring what areas of your life need a strong yes from you, what situations call for a clear no, and where it is necessary that you admit that, at this time, you do not know what your answer is but you are willing to stay with the discomfort of not knowing until your yes or no surfaces.

YES, NO, MAYBE SO?

Life changes are fostered by our willingness to make new choices. The wheel of life is propelled by the sometimes imperceptible choices we make.

If it were possible to map our own histories by recalling and documenting all the times in our past when we acted on a yes when we really meant no and stopped action with a no when we really meant yes, we would have an accurate account of how we landed at some of the confusing and problematic places we find ourselves in today.

Some of us are automatic yes machines. We say yes to involvements without thinking and often find ourselves far afield of our own life purposes and goals as a result of the detour. Some of us are automatic no machines.

We habitually say no to invitations, ideas, adventures, and opportunities out of the habit of keeping a *Keep Off The Grass* sign firmly implanted around our established and set ways of experiencing our lives.

One of the benefits of learning to open to and access our intuitive guidance is that we begin to discover that we have a storehouse of untapped personal wisdom available.

This inner knowing of untapped guidance is the gold that has been forged from the painful and powerful consequences we have already endured as the price of making incomplete, hasty, frivolous, blind, and sometimes disastrous choices at earlier times.

It takes a certain strength of spirit to become a powerful decision-maker. The best decisions are made with an almost muscular, clean, fierce precision. All aspects of ourselves align behind one clear, bold step and when that happens, there is a visceral satisfaction that energizes us to the core.

That kind of intense clarity is a true gift from the gods. More often, we are merely foot soldiers, trudging through the swampy and murky waters of day-to-day reality with a vague and often unsettling unsurety about where we are going, how we got here, and why we are making or avoiding the decisions we currently face.

All decisions are made on insufficient evidence; therefore searching outside of ourselves for the one perfect, good, right decision that will yield all benefits and no prices is merely an infantile attempt to sidestep fully participating, owning, authoring, and taking responsibility for the lives we are choosing.

Decision-making is an art, not a science. **The ability to decide is the fuel that drives responsible living.** The term decision-making is actually too small to house all of the ingredients necessary to venture out well-equipped to choose and decide our own fate.

In our childhoods, we were pushed, prodded, scolded, shamed, manipulated, controlled, and coerced into making decisions before we were ready. The polite term for that is socialization. Most of us found ourselves powerless and lost as children and, as a result, the business of choosing responsibly can seem like treacherous and dangerous business today.

Therefore, we hesitate, over-think, over-analyze, worry, and wait for the feeling of total confidence, surety, safety, and security that is wishful thinking and could only happen if we spent our lives cocooned in the back of our closets hiding under a blanket.

Discernment is the love child birthed from the marriage of what we know and what we feel. Feelings include contemplation, emotional sincerity, a willingness to forge an intimate working relationship with both yes and no, and inner listening.

> *True knowing requires us to respect the unknown, allowing our fears, apprehensions and inadequacies to lend their voices to the decision process. Our intuition supplies access to our deeper longings, unfulfilled dreams, and desires. Our orphaned and abandoned losses and sorrows must also be welcomed home.*

When we decide to stop our frantic running and stand still and stand up to our fears and failures, we can begin the process of opening the floodgates to receive moment-to-moment guidance and small, step-by-step direction from our inspirational Divine Source.

> *When we decide to consciously allow the stream of well-being to flow through our decisions, our intentions, and our every thought; inner inspiration and outer right-action fall in love. And that love of the life we are creating begins to dance.*

An Equal Partnership

Yes and No were having an argument about who was more valuable. Yes started, being the more open of the two, by expressing how exciting it is to have so many varied experiences.

"My value is clearly superior in the scheme of things. Without me, nothing would happen. I venture out into the world exuberantly. My days are filled with excitement and new experiences. I open my arms and embrace life and living. What could be better than that?"

"Well, first," said No, "safety would be better, and firm ground to stand on. Self-control and control of my environment. The room to hear myself think and the ability to conserve my energy for the things that are most important to me."

"You make me dizzy with your endless activity, your lack of discernment, and disregard for consistent, organized, and methodical actions coupled with your total disregard for boundaries. I fear for *your* safety. I never know what to expect when I am around you." With hardly a breath in between, No continued on.

"Another thing that bothers me is that you say yes to everyone and yes to every experience. Yes to life, yes to love, yes to adventure. Then the next thing I know, the person whose mouth you jumped out of is crouched in a mangled mess under the covers whimpering and calling my name. And to make matters worse, they don't do it at a decent hour. It is always at around 3:00 AM. They wake me out of a sound night's sleep moaning 'No, No, No. Why did I do it? No. No. Not again!"

"You get all the glory and leave the hardest parts for me. When I am called on duty it almost always requires me to save somebody from potential abuse or to salvage a disastrous situation."

Now, if the truth were known, No actually relishes his job and gets a thrill every time he takes his stand. He loves the feeling of strength and self-containment and that moment of pure silence that is created right after he shows up. The only place that is difficult for him is with children. They are his least favorite assignment. He shouldn't complain because the work in that area is steady and is what pays the bills, yet it is tedious and repetitive work and he gets little to no respect.

He knows that if he is going to win this argument, his best bet is to stick with the topic of adults.

"I am the voice of responsibility and authority. 'No, I will not stand for this. No, that will not work for me. No, I am not interested. No thank you. No, I do not want that.' Without me, people would have no power. They would be wimpy people-pleasers with their energy scattered to the four winds. They would be mindless, operating on automatic pilot, yelling: "Yes, Yes, Yes. I am so excited. Bring on life, I can't wait. Yippee!" It makes me cringe just thinking of the world without me."

Yes is starting to get mad. He hates talking to No because he often finds himself feeling invalidated and vulnerable around him. Everything he holds dear, No considers trite. No is formidable to argue with because he often takes a defensive, judgmental stance.

"No, I think you have too big a hold on the spirit of most people. You have been whispering no in their ears for such a long time, you have killed their spark, their zest for life. Left unchecked, you are a killer. You kill imagination, curiosity, and exuberance."

"I am getting sick of it. I am going to double my efforts with the children I know because I have seen you almost immobilized when faced with a five-year-old that wants to do something. When their natural enthusiasm is pitted against your negativity, there is no contest. And an adult with their enthusiasm re-kindled is unstoppable."

"I am anything but trite. The real problem is that by the time you have bombarded someone throughout their entire life, they have no fire left. Without a core connection with their spirit, people use me, Yes, as a distraction to keep busy so that they don't have to confront their own emptiness and confusion."

"They are disconnected from themselves because you run their internal life. You make them wrong. You invalidate their inner yearnings. You kill their budding new ideas with your negativity. Then they use me to pursue a meaningless, purposeless life trying to find some external thrills because their internal life is so barren."

No is shocked. At his core, No is dignified and courageous. The comments Yes just made point out how he has become caught up in a web of negativity.

"I guess I am, all too often, used to express people's built-up resentment, anger, and defensiveness. I now realize that I have become small and petty myself. I had no idea how hard my actions have made your job."

"I am willing to partner with you with the intention of helping people to find their heart's desires, your arena, and then they can use my skills to establish appropriate boundaries that conserve their energy for the most productive and fulfilling uses."

This turn of events was thrilling to Yes because he realized that building a loving, respectful partnership with No would allow him to fulfill his true destiny.

From this point on, Yes and No agreed to work together using their individual powers to create full, rich, and rewarding lives for anyone who has the courage to embrace the use of both Yes and No wholeheartedly.

Open To

If this door calls to you, it is important to remember to detach from a results-only, bottom-line focus and instead, place yourself in new situations as a novice. Allow yourself to step back and surrender the lead in favor of learning to be receptive and responsive rather than being the doer, the decider, and the expert in charge.

THE COURAGE TO BE OPEN

The health and growth of our relationships hinges on our skill in the art of openness. I call openness an art to distinguish it from pronouncements made in hopes that words alone will deliver the positive results that guarantee that we will look good and be right and in control.

Openness is a powerful force that must be treated with respect and used responsibly. Blurting out the first thought that randomly bubbles to the surface is a sure indicator of our lack of understanding of the power of true openness to set in motion the fulfillment of our heart's longing to be connected and in communion with like-minded others.

When we decide to risk being open with another, we set sail on a journey into uncharted territory. There is no guarantee that our self-disclosure will be received, heard, respected, accepted, or understood fully by another. Because the results are so unpredictable, why would any thinking person take the risk of opening their private, secure inner world to someone else?

The answer lies within the definition of open. Open is defined as: *not* shut or blocked up; allowing passage in or out; without restrictions; available; exposed; frank and sincere; clear, unobstructed space; to set open; to uncover; to give access to; to become open; to begin; a beginning; an opportunity.

There is an unspoken agreement in our society that goes something like this: "Let's be open. You first." When we are reticent to disclose anything but name, rank, and serial number, we take up a place in the ranks of the terrible, slow, boring army of the interpersonally cautious.

The motivation to be safe from judgment, criticism, and emotional harm from others is understandable but, taken to extremes, ensures that the joy of discovery, the mystery and the magic of truly knowing another, will stay forever out of our grasp.

Wishing and hoping that someone will someday soon appear in your life bringing gifts of warmth, camaraderie, and love is a wonderful fantasy but an unlikely reality. It would be like trying to warm yourself at a fireplace that has no wood and isn't lit, yet sitting in front of it demanding incessantly: "Give me fire and I promise that as soon as you do, I will put in the wood."

Our decision to elevate our understanding of the dynamics of openness sets the stage for genuine opportunities to create new beginnings. Often, in our important relationships, we are afraid we will expose ourselves too much and also are afraid that we won't expose ourselves enough. This ambivalence about speaking of what is most significant to us is very common.

What is most important to share is often also the area where we are most vulnerable. We all conceal much of ourselves from others and therefore travel 'incognito' to some degree. Because of our fears and insecurities, we hide the very things that most need to be discussed.

In our culture, we commonly have two types of problems with our feelings. On one hand, we may be unaware of our emotions. On the other hand, feelings sometimes surge through us with such force that reason becomes impotent. We are, therefore, either blind to or blinded by our emotions.

Our emotions are key to the quality of our relationships because they help define and shape what we value. Our feelings are a fundamental part of our motivation and help determine our direction and purpose in life.

Openness is an art and it is day labor. It requires an expenditure of energy to sidestep our passion for appearing perfect, in favor of surrendering to the intuitive call of our heart's intelligence and the quest to open new vistas in our lives.

If we are out of touch with ourselves, then it is impossible to touch others. The paradox is that we are each solely responsible for the quality of our lives, but to have any meaning, our lives must include relationships.

We all have certain basic needs in common whether we admit it or not. We need to be wanted, welcomed, safe, nourished, seen, heard, included, and communicated with. When we take on the challenge of treating others with respect and acceptance, we meet and come together in a spirit of communion where everyone benefits. The result is renewal, regeneration, and stimulating energy gains.

The investment? We must be willing to be open with ourselves and admit, acknowledge, own, and manage our personal insecurities instead of hiding them or making others pay for our unfulfilled needs.

Opening to the treasure of our own intuitive guidance and direction helps to set us free. When we no longer fear our inner world then contact and connection with others becomes a delightful luxury that allows our authenticity to grow and genuine relationships to flourish.

CELEBRATING THE UNKNOWN

Often it seems that life will make sense if we can get enough answers neatly lined up in a row. However, if it were possible to have all the answers, where would that put us? Would we be elevated to the status of expert and be protected from disasters as a result?

I once heard a speaker who was introduced as being an expert in his field. He took the microphone and said that he always gets nervous when he is billed as an expert. "When you break down the word expert, it isn't as complimentary as I once thought. You see, an ex is a has-been and a spurt is a drip under pressure."

What if we turn our focus away from storing answers in favor of elevating the value of not knowing?

Try it on for a moment. "I don't know. I don't know what will happen tomorrow. I don't know the answer. I don't have an instant, ready-made response."

I don't already know who you are based upon your age, your address, your title, or your marital status. I can't begin to know your depth. Your depth of pain. Your depth of life experiences. Your depth of knowledge. Your depth of abilities. Your depth of fears, wishes, hopes, and dreams.

If we use our time together trying to establish our superiority by proving how much we know, we miss an opportunity to truly learn from each other and about each other.

Claiming expertise seems to be a national pastime. It amazes me how often I hear quick, fast pronouncements of simplistic, one-size-fits-all answers to complex situations, volunteered aggressively without even being asked for.

There is so much thrown at us daily that doesn't have a quick answer. We become passive observers to horrible tragedies through the nightly news that can leave us deeply disturbed because we are simply witnesses to the pain of others with no ability to comfort or help.

My heart clutches and I turn my face away as I listen to an interview and feel the pain of the mother of a boy who went on a killing spree. "I don't know if I'll ever be able to close my eyes again," she says. In response, the reporter unblinkingly asks her another insensitive, cold, strategic question. Watching her, I know why we pretend to know more than we do.

We do it for protection because when we say "I don't know" it opens us up. It makes us vulnerable and easily get-to-able. It gives others a chance to jump in and try to fill us up with their answers. And the beat goes on.

I won't let you see my vulnerability. You won't let me see yours. We are at a stalemate and our lives get colder and more isolated and more predictable. We become more emotionally distant from others and ourselves.

Distanced from our bigger questions. Distanced from our transformational curiosity and alert innocence. We settle for the Jerry Springer variety of petty, base, voyeuristic curiosity instead.

> *It takes courage to stay in the questioning process. It takes alert, awake intention to lead an adventurous life. We must honor our unknowns. Our undiscovered attributes. Our budding dreams and wishes, hopes, and desires.*

Newly-born ideas and visions must be nurtured and loved. They need to be parented until they can stand on their own. "I have a new idea and it is in the I-don't-know-what-it-will-become stage."

"I do not know what I'm going to do about this situation but I reserve the right to find my own answers." "I have no response to that question." "I don't want your input right now. The idea is too fragile and new to be critiqued."

It takes courage to say these things but say them you must. To your mate. To your friends. To your loved ones. To yourself. To whoever is unwittingly killing your passion for the unknown.

> *Guard your wondering, questioning, and curious self with a passion fit for a mother tiger protecting her cubs. Stand up for your process of becoming.*

Don't allow yourself to be pressed, slotted, and formed into a static, predictable, contained, easily understood, packaged, and labeled life.

Beware of allowing your own insecurities to turn the adventure of your life into an accident. An accident of sameness and mediocrity instead of the intriguing, on-going adventure it is meant to be.

Strengthen

If this door has your attention, it may be that you are too committed to fulfilling others' expectations and have dropped the ball in relation to yourself. If this is so, take on the task of making and keeping commitments to yourself, by yourself, thereby strengthening your self-trust. When you trust yourself sufficiently, you strengthen your ability to make discerning life choices.

LIFE MANAGEMENT 101

Saying yes creates energy movement out into the world. Yes is a door opener. Saying no puts perimeters around our lives, our energy, and ourselves. No slows down, closes down, shuts down the show. No is a door-closer.

We must have affinity for the right use of both yes and no to manage our multidimensional lives successfully.

Creating safety and security means opening some doors, saying yes, while closing others, saying no. Stabilizing often requires liberal use of no until we have come back home enough to find our grounding. Stretching requires an opening up again and that usually means generous use of yes.

Here is a three-word formula for self-management: Secure. Stabilize. Stretch. These three S's supply a perfect guideline for knowing when to say yes and when to say no.

Growth and progress depend mightily on our ability to secure enough information and support to create safety, plus the ability to be patient and still while we stabilize and then, when we are sure-footed, we can take the risks required to stretch out of our comfort zones.

The tricky part is that our lives are multifaceted. One area may be screaming for safety and security while other aspects of our lives are closing down from lack of stimulation.

For example, perhaps your work life is on the grow. You are taking on new challenges every day. It is exciting, simulating, and stressful. Energy-demanding. You are in the fast lane. Your career is in the stretch mode.

So much time is devoted to work, however, that your personal life is nonexistent. You may have to begin to pay rent for the space your clothes are taking up at the cleaners. Then there are the unscheduled dental appointments, haircuts, car maintenance, house repairs, and all the nonwork relationships that have been lingering on the back burner to-do list in your mind. Everything is demanding maintenance attention.

You are an automatic yes machine when it comes to work projects. You are on automatic no regarding the personal. You are off-balance, out of balance, lopsided, one-sided. Off course.

It takes flexibility and awareness to shift back and forth between yes and no.

When you find yourself in the yes mode and your energy is rushing out fast and furiously, take notice.

All stretch with no maintenance ultimately creates insecurity. The underpinnings of your security base may begin to unravel, leaving you high and dry. Like a hummingbird with wings flapping furiously but with no place to land.

⌒ **Secure. Stabilize. Stretch.**

Apply these three S's to the important areas of your life and once you have done a needs assessment, take the right actions necessary to allow yourself to have a place to stand firmly; from that secure position spread your wings and fly.

GRACE AND GRIT

It takes courage to stand up to life, face our fears, and take the actions necessary to handle our responsibilities.

It is high praise to be labeled as a responsible and independent person and it is demeaning and dismissive to be judged as irresponsible and therefore by inference, incompetent, untrustworthy, inept, over-lookable, and a loser rather than a winner.

No one in his or her right mind sets out to be a loser in the game of life. As children we get the notion that when we grow up and take our rightful place as adults we will no longer be vulnerable.

All the stories of the heroes from history prove that if you stand up, no matter what, you will ultimately triumph and through Herculean feats of inner and outer strength, you will survive.

The stories usually skim over the times of confusion, doubt, despair, grief, pain, and self-loathing simply because those experiences muddy up the water and take the punch out of the motivational message that, through true grit, the world's treasures are there for the taking for the man or woman who will grab the handle of courage and fight the good fight with no thought of retreat.

Let's back up here for a moment and explore some not-so-obvious pitfalls inherent in this "I will survive," "I am woman hear me roar," and "I did it my way" stance towards life.

If it is good to be independent, it stands to reason that it would be bad to be dependent. Total independence would require a fierce and aggressive approach to securing our fortress against any enemies who could usurp our invincible personal power. Dependence would require submissiveness and the willingness to surrender to circumstances outside of our control.

Dependence and submission, when held as negatives, become the doorway through which we enter onto the slippery slide of passive victimhood. We are done in by life and we are pathetic.

In those quiet, dark moments when our life is stuck, stopped, and diminished through unforeseen circumstances, wrong choices, and/or a kick from fate, we are thrown into frozen panic and despair and shamefully take on the mantle of victimhood.

We berate ourselves for being a pathetic, non-functioning loser/victim and feel humiliated in our own eyes as well as the eyes of the world.

If we are able to be honest, we have each felt these feelings and thought these thoughts at some time in our lives.

So, according to these choices, we are either a victim or we are responsible. We are passive or aggressive. We are dependent or independent. We are a loser or a winner. These statements are only true to the degree that we live in a made-up, conceptual, static, black and white, good or bad, right or wrong world of frozen polar opposites.

As we loosen our hold on our either/or thinking, new awareness begins to surface.

As children we were dependent. Since we made it to adulthood, we know that we received at least enough sustenance to survive. We were sustained through no creation of our own. We received and we grew. We showed up and we thrived.

Therefore independence cannot be the top of the mountain. It cannot be the way and the truth to creating a full and rich life. It is part of the story. Just not the whole story.

Here is a well-kept secret that, once known, could change your life as you are presently experiencing it: Striving, fighting, wrestling life to the ground, grabbing life and extracting all that you can locks you solidly into the other side of passive victimhood. You become an active victim.

You take on the impossible, you never surrender, and you continually push the boulder up the hill. You become a human gerbil on the treadmill of life. Though you are not a passive victim, you become a tragic victim of endless striving.

All that effort and you become unable to relax, to enjoy, to love and be loved, to delight, to invite, to revel in the joy of your creations. You become a human doing on automatic pilot devoid of the spontaneity and wonder that was once a part of the child that is trapped inside of your invulnerable adult facade.

There is another way.

Make a new decision to thrive. Be willing to surrender and also be willing to stand up. Be dependent and be independent and then you can grow into the skill of interdependence. Learn what is right action for you so that you know when to hold and when to fold.

Begin the journey within in earnest. Instead of exclusively looking outside of yourself to see what you can get from the world, look inside to see what you are really made of.

Find what is exceptional about you. **Begin to realize the little-known fact that what makes you exceptional is often what makes you lonely.**

⁓ *Own your pain and give up your long suffering. Keep your strengths and grit and court your softness and inner guidance through the grace of intuition.*

Instead of continuing to struggle, take up the fight for a new loveliness of a life of your own making that allows you to thrive, nurtured and sustained by the gifts birthed from the marriage of grace and grit.

Wisdom's Home

Wisdom grows from life experiences. Tough times often teach us more about life and ourselves than when things go smoothly and easily.

A problem occurs when we are attached to the painful memories and cannot let go of them. Therefore, the thoughts and feelings about past upsets remain no matter what we do.

Perhaps they stay because we forgot to glean the wisdom from the experience. We forgot to focus on the lessons learned, the new people that came into our lives, the love and care that we received, or the new doors that were opened as a result.

Can you recall a painful life experience that forced you to re-evaluate and change the direction of your life? Did you grow? Are you more able to be discerning in your choices of people and situations in which you now get involved? Are you more forgiving and accepting of yourself? Are you more able to be compassionate? Are you more in touch with your innate strength of character and your personal power? Are you less gullible and more discriminating? Are you better able to see, cope, and accept reality?

All of the above are Wisdom's gifts.

The point here is that we don't have to like the experiences but it is necessary to access and own the wisdom to allow the painful memories to fade into the background.

You have already experienced the pain. You have paid that price. So why not accept the benefit of increased wisdom and give yourself the permission you have earned and allow yourself to move on?

Looking at our lives from this point of view, we finally can begin to notice that we have a stockpile of wisdom ready to be called on whenever we choose.

So let's imagine you are visiting Wisdom's home today. Your wisdom may live high on a mountaintop or deep in the ocean or somewhere else. Simply allow your mind to take you to the place where your wisdom resides.

And now, see yourself standing at Wisdom's front door. Knock and Wisdom will be there to open the door and welcome you inside.

As you enter, take some time to get a feel for the opulence of Wisdom's house and how well the wisdom part of you is living. Wisdom may be a bit surprised to see you or perhaps this is not your first visit after all.

You probably are a frequent visitor but didn't know it on a conscious level until now.

Sometimes we visit Wisdom only when we want to get information to help a friend. We forget that Wisdom is also there to assist in any decisions we need to make for ourselves.

We can get in the habit, from early training, of assuming that only experts and authorities are the holders of wisdom. We mistakenly learn to bypass our own knowledge in favor of collecting information elsewhere.

Now that you know where Wisdom resides, think of a situation that you are facing right now in your life. Ask your wisdom for its best shot. Go to your own wisdom base before you go to anyone else.

> *Often all it takes to trust our own judgment is practice. We must give ourselves permission to believe that our own knowledge is valuable and a true asset.*

In no time at all, it becomes a newly formed habit and enjoyable to take responsibility and authority for all our life experiences. "Been there, done that" can then be rephrased to "been there, understand that." This is how personal power is built.

Personal power comes to us as a result of knowledge and understanding based on our digestion and integration of all of our unique life experiences; the published and the private, the huge heart-hurts, and the small slights and hidden wounds. They each have their own wisdom attached.

> *Personal power, once earned, can never be taken away.*

The heart-softening compassion that comes from life's trials and tribulations accepted and integrated into the fabric of our being allows us to grow into a substantial person with a worthy contribution to make.

Wisdom is bought from the coin of heart joys and heart-hurts woven into the fabric of our being so that we can finally abandon the impossible lusting after perfection in favor of fully embracing the vibrant and compelling coat of authenticity.

CHAPTER 7   THRIVING: LIVING FULLY AND LOVING WELL

Success and Fulfillment met at a cocktail party.

It was rare for Success to attend this type of function. He usually only made time for events that directly furthered his goals. This event was a fundraiser for a worthy charity. In a rare moment of hesitation, he committed himself to show up and felt obligated to follow through.

He was mingling. In every conversation, it was second nature to him to leave no doubt that he was an accomplished business professional. After all, what else is there?

In his experience, there are only two positions in life…better than or less than. Superior or inferior. He decided at an early age to set his sights on the top of the mountain and never looked back.

Sure, he had his setbacks. They simply fueled the fire to use his intellect to rise to the challenge. As a result of his stance, he had weathered his share of disappointments and losses without missing a beat.

Pushing, striving, and keeping his eye firmly planted on the goal had really paid off. His image of himself was firmly established and, dare he say it, life was actually demanding less of him all the time.

As a matter of fact, if anything was making him a bit uneasy, it was the fact that he was already the winner almost everywhere.

I say almost, because Success was rather unlucky in love. Intimate relationships were not his strong suit. He vaguely remembered the first time he fell in love. He was sixteen. She felt like poetry and loving her was as natural as being attracted to ocean waves or the crackling of a warm fire. He opened his heart to her and knew they would be together forever.

The painful details of their break-up were too buried in the past to be recalled, but the bottom line was, he got his heart broken.

He learned early that love was too costly. That was when he decided to strategically plan his life and monitor his investments, whether they involved love or money.

Yes, he had relationships. Some lasted longer than others but the day always came when they wanted too much from him or they asked too little and he overpowered them.

He decided that many, short-term, superficial relationships suited him better. He wined, dined, and charmed a variety of very attractive, intelligent women. Actually, not to brag, but he could get the attention of anyone he wanted. He was in demand.

Fulfillment arrived a bit later then she had planned. On her way to the event, the sun was just setting and it was exquisite. She pulled her car off to the side of the road and marveled at the kaleidoscope of colors that was shifting and changing right before her eyes. Her heart felt full as she drank in the abundant beauty of the sky and water surrounding her.

The fundraiser was for one of her favorite charities and, as she put her car in gear, she wondered for a moment what the evening would bring.

She smiled to herself as she remembered how nervous and apprehensive she used to feel when she was required to show up at social events. She never understood the point of cocktail party conversation and didn't feel that she measured up to the expectations all around her; therefore, social interactions were a burden rather than a pleasure.

A major turning point was when she realized that the pressure she felt was ninety-nine percent self-imposed. That was when she set out to learn how to become comfortable in her own skin rather than trying to control how others saw her.

She was at a stage in her life where she no longer worried about what people thought of her. Her attention was on who she would meet that would spark her curiosity, feed her mind, delight her heart.

She noticed Success right away. He had a certain presence about him. He took up room and had an aura of confidence firmly established around him.

As she greeted people she knew, Success became aware of her. He felt drawn to her almost against his will.

There was something different about her. She exuded a sensation of warmth and approachability without being overdone. Actually, she was more understated than flamboyant, yet when she was talking to someone, she seemed totally engaged.

He managed to position himself close enough to her so that it seemed natural that they introduce themselves. He was a bit taken aback by the solidity of her handshake and the steadiness of her eye contact.

What transferred was a feeling of strength and sensitivity, warmth and substance, and gentleness and kindness without a trace of weakness. *She's not to be taken lightly*, he thought.

They exchanged names and stood there rather awkwardly. For the first time in quite a while, Success felt self-conscious. He asked her what she did.

Fulfillment smiled gently. She looked him in the eyes and said: "On my way here, I saw the most beautiful sunset. It's still replaying in the corners of my mind."

She was unpredictable and unrehearsed. Success found himself both unsettled and intrigued. He actually didn't care what she did for a living. He was only asking because business was his strong suit. Somehow, it didn't seem necessary to establish his professional position. His accomplishments didn't need to be dragged out in front of her. Fulfillment seemed to see him and accept him without reservations.

He almost felt the way he used to when he was sixteen and first fell in love. But even better, because he now had enough accomplishments to know his capabilities and to know that he was already successful according to the world's terms.

Fulfillment was immediately intrigued as she made eye contact with Success. She was used to meeting new people, having pleasant conversation, and moving on without a ripple of true connection being kindled, since light and superficial exchanges are the norm.

Her first impression of Success as a force and a presence transferred strongly as they shook hands. She bypassed answering the question of what she did and instead followed her deeper inclination to tell him about something that was closer to her heart at that moment; the magnificence of the sunset that was still warming her sense of wonder and delight.

She was pleased that Success, though obviously charismatic, was able to receive what she said without demanding or commanding that she stay on track with cocktail conversation.

She felt comfortable in his presence, seen and heard in a way that didn't happen very often. Though their conversation was marked with awkwardness, it was more because of the limitless possibilities that seem to show up when enough inner solidity, self-knowledge, and self-acceptance come together to encourage authenticity rather than posturing.

Maybe there is something beyond better than, less than superior, inferior, independent, dependent, role-oriented, and predictable ways of relating.

Maybe there is a vast territory, an unexplored space that lives beyond restricted definitions, where genuine connection and real, trusting, respectful, interdependent relationships are born.

Perhaps, with a bit of courage, a true friendship and partnership will continue to grow from the spark that has been ignited between Success and Fulfillment.

Mutual Respect

Each of us, whether man or woman, has both masculine energy and feminine energy available to us.

Masculine energy is active, dynamic, forward-moving, out-flowing, and able to manifest tangible results in the external world. Feminine energy is open, receptive, inner directed, deeply-seated, experientially based, circular, and attuned to nuances and feelings with an intention to nurture our ability to be well with who we are.

The marriage of our masculine and feminine energy is the union that provides each of us the opportunity to be a human being who produces external results that match our clear intentions.

Makes sense, doesn't it? Then how come it is so difficult to get these two energies to even show up in the same town at the same time? Never mind having them take on the daunting task of working in a full partnership with each other.

I suspect some of the problem has to do with too small a definition of what it means to enter into a marriage. Coupled with that is a lack of expanded knowledge and acceptance of the reality that both men and women are supposed to actively own and use both dynamic and receptive energy.

Owning all of our energies equips us with the ability to have both personal power and position power available to us. When both energies work in tandem, we can fully participate and carve out a productive place for ourselves in our world.

Rigid role identification keeps us stuck in "blue is for boys" and "pink is for girls" mentality. The me Tarzan/you Jane definition of what a man or woman is supposed to be creates lives that are stuck, stagnant, small, deadening, and unworkable.

It might be time to call an emergency meeting with your masculine and feminine energy to assess the health or disease of their relationship. It may be a big surprise for them to find out that they are supposed to have a relationship with each other.

Most of us use the tag team approach to partnership. This is when either your masculine or your feminine energy is calling the shots but they hardly, if ever, cooperate or collaborate.

If you are the constant producer of a whirlwind of activity and a generator of more, bigger, and better results but your ability to relate to anyone or anything that is warm and breathing, including yourself, is dried up and brittle, it is time for you to open up to, accept, and surrender into the arms of your feminine energy.

Court her until your soul has been nourished and nurtured back to life. Resolve to include her in your decision-making by learning to respect your deep-seated need and unexpressed, unacknowledged desire for more tenderness, kindness, and self-love to round out your self-definition.

If you find yourself in touch with your full range of emotions and you have a rich inner life but can't seem to make your presence known, your voice heard, or your needs met, it is time to seek out your masculine energy.

If you feel you are slowly sinking down into disappointment and despair, it is time to have a serious talk with your protective and dynamic energy.

Let your masculine energy know that when he sees you raising your hands up it is because you are drowning, not waving. Let him know that you need his ability to focus, decide, and commit to specific performable tasks and actions to help move you both forward.

Thank him for being willing to provide the action steps and outline the task focus necessary to manifest your dreams. Resolve to allow him to do his job of bringing your rich inner experiences and creative ideas into form and out into the light of day.

When we open to all of our energies, we place our feet firmly on our unique life path. We can then get ready, willing, and able to move forward, with both our receptive and active energies fully committed and involved.

The Courage To Be Happy

There are two basic ways to view our lives and ourselves. We can see life either as a problem to be solved or as a reality to be experienced. Each point of view has its pitfalls as well as its benefits.

If I am operating exclusively from the position that life is a problem, I will only be present and engaged when I have a problem or you have a problem, or the business or the family or the world has a problem.

The weather will be a problem, earning a living will be problematic, and the topic of all my conversations will be devoted to describing, discussing, and dissecting whatever problem currently has my attention.

Some of the obvious drawbacks to this point of view are that we become tethered to the never-ending treadmill of mental stress, strain, and overwork. We become overwhelmed by our daily responsibilities accomplished to the tune of 'life is hard and then we die'.

Our emotional range becomes severely limited to varying degrees of fear that we won't be able to solve the problems or anger and frustration that we have to stand up to yet another crisis.

When we approach life as a reality to be experienced instead of a problem to be solved, we add a wide lens to our way of seeing. We allow the presence of our emotions, whether happy, sad, fearful, angry, disappointed, or vacant, to inform our responses to whatever is currently happening in our lives.

From this point of view, whatever is, is. There is nothing to fix or figure out, either with ourselves or anyone else. Life comes to us and we to it as an unfolding interaction happening moment by moment.

The main stumbling blocks to this point of view are pretense, misinformation, and wishful thinking caused by a sometimes severe case of denial and unwillingness to confront the real issues in our lives.

What do I mean?

We all want to be happy, healthy, safe, secure, well cared for, cherished, and loved. We all have experienced unhappiness, varying degrees of sickness, insecurity, feeling unsafe, neglected, devalued, rejected, and unloved. Given the choice, we would all pick happy. As a matter of fact, we are all trying to create happiness in the best way we know how.

The 'life is a problem to be solved' approach acknowledges that many experiences that come our way don't feel good. They don't bring happiness. We are required to stand up to life. We must confront, wrestle with, mold, shape, and form a workable environment for ourselves and those we love. This is part of reality. It just isn't all of it.

When we develop the courage to be happy despite the heart-hurts, trials, tribulations, and challenges that we encounter, we give ourselves permission to open to life as a multifaceted reality to be experienced. We allow in some softness, support, excitement, and fun so that life doesn't always have to be the bad guy.

The 'life is a reality to be experienced' point of view is play-acting because the rough, tough, and edgy aspects of our lives are denied, ignored, and glossed over. Choosing to deny that it is raining because we only like sunshine is delusional.

Traditional or New Age thinking that sets up dogma to bypass our fears, angers, apprehensions, and challenges is simply a childish and silly attempt to grab the happiness pill and eat it once and for all as a safeguard and protection from any further pain.

Life is both a problem to be solved and a reality to be experienced. How we see it depends on our state of mind and the degree that we are able to be honest with ourselves.

> *Life mastery comes from our ability to be recep-*
> *tive to all of our feelings and to be flexible enough*
> *to know when to stand up and fight, when to*
> *surrender, when to drop back and let go, and*
> *when to dance.*

When we continue to uncover and discover our true motives and become increasingly visible to ourselves, we open to the opportunity to be courageously happy with a life that is fierce with reality.

Four Life-Changing Attitudes

There are four attitudes that hold the key to transforming the way we are presently experiencing our lives and lead to much greater happiness and peace of mind.

1.   **The first attitude is respect.** When we conduct our lives with an attitude of respect we bring consideration, regard, civility, courtesy, politeness, attention, and reverence into our energetic field. This point of view allows us to bypass the rough, crude, rude, negative thinking that drains energy and fosters defensiveness and confrontational interpersonal interactions that leave us upset and disappointed.

2.   **The second attitude is harmony.** When we adopt an intention to bring harmony into our lives, we validate the idea of unity. Community, cooperation, caring, mutual understanding, synergy, collaboration, and ease flow from this way of seeing. When we actively seek out ways that we are similar to others instead of different, we move away from isolation, anxiety, and the fear that "they are out to get me and I need to defend myself against attack."

3.   **The third attitude is gratitude.** In order to be grateful for something, we must first assign value to it. If we don't value it we can't and won't be grateful. Here is the magical part. It is so easy to take for granted the wonderful aspects of our lives, in favor of striving and relentlessly driving ourselves toward the creation of more, bigger, and better. When we stop and evaluate our lives through the lens of being grateful, guess what happens? We see a life full of value right here and right now. It is therefore worthwhile to intentionally take stock of the valuable people, valuable experiences, and valuable possessions we presently have if we want to bring more satisfaction into our lives. Gratitude is attitude adjustment number three.

4. **The fourth attitude is praise.** Praise is the mother of beauty. Why? Think about it. Would you praise and compliment something that you think is ugly? Probably not. So when we adopt an attitude of praise and validation, we must be actively looking for and seeking out beauty. If we want more beauty, we must figure out how to see more beauty by increasing our self-acceptance and our acceptance of others. Seeking beauty opens the door for curiosity, love, kindness, and the lightening up of our critical judgments. Praise is attitude adjustment number four.

When we embrace and exercise the healing power in all respectful, harmonious, grateful, and complimentary actions, we can begin to watch the magic as we break open and transform our habitual, stilted, and limited ways of seeing ourselves and those around us.

Your Happiness Quotient

Happiness is a state of mind. The question is how do we get it? What triggers the experience of being happy? What is it about happiness that makes it so elusive?

If you take a moment to reflect on your own experience of Happiness, there are a few aspects of her personality that come immediately to light. Happiness seems a bit unstable. As a friend, she is unreliable, inconsistent, and flighty. Frankly, she doesn't score high in either loyalty or accountability either.

As a matter of fact, she is downright self-centered and difficult to please for any length of time. I know this sounds like blatant character assassination but we need to have a heart-to-heart talk about her so that we can clearly assess whether it is even worth spending the time and energy to court her into our lives.

She may simply be too much trouble and, if that is the case, though disappointing, at least we can stop striving in that direction and settle for an experience that is safer and more secure; like mild contentment for example.

Though Happiness is quite well-known and widely accepted in many social circles, she comes from a family background that includes some sketchy characters. Though everyone is an individual in his or her own right, early influences can play a part in character building and therefore should be taken into consideration.

Spontaneity, Passion, Zest for living, Exuberance, and Gaiety are direct relatives of hers. To be fair, she does have a brother who has made quite a name for himself in spiritual circles by channeling his excesses into well-intentioned Enthusiasm. Since the word enthusiasm literally means "filled with God" this does seem to lift him above reproach.

In general, though, Happiness seems to be a bit of a wild child. She shows up on your doorstep with sunlight streaming through her hair and winds of delight whistling around her. A pink light settles in down and around your daily life so that it all seems friendlier. Nothing is different and yet everything seems easier and all right.

No wonder we long for a visit from Happiness and are willing to ignore the fact that when she ups and leaves it is devastating and makes us wish we had never met her, the loss is so great.

Once Happiness has visited your life, you are never the same. If she is a consistent houseguest, some self-congratulations are called for here. It means that you have mastered certain skills that allow her to come often and stay long.

Happiness lives on her own timeline. She cannot and will not tolerate commands, demands, or heavy-handed control measures. She will only respond to a light, accepting touch. She is highly curious and changes her mind often so it is pointless to try to pin her down with contracts or commitments. She is a free agent.

Happiness requires us to let go of our tight hold that keeps us stifled, controlled, and emotionally restricted. We must be willing to open our minds and hearts to the unpredictable, uncontrollable, and unknowable aspects of life by easing up on our need to know, to be sure, and to be right.

There is one big secret about Happiness that, once you know, will give you the key to a lifelong friendship with her. I have waited this long to tell you because I want to make sure that you are sincere about wanting Happiness in your life and you are capable and worthy of her friendship.

This will take a bit of explaining, so stay with me.

I am sure you are familiar with the phrase: Misery loves company. The truth is that Misery does love company and his main companion is Happiness. I know this may be hard to grasp but hear me out.

Misery and Happiness are soulmates. He fell in love with her long ago and will never let her go. She wouldn't think of leaving him either. They are so secure in their relationship that each carries out their life purpose individually and then reconnect at the appropriate times to keep their relationship alive and well.

Now, don't just take my word for this. See for yourself. Recall a time in your life when you were particularly happy. Now push the memory further until you find the edge when happiness turned into something else. Recall how it seemed that happiness started to slip away and was replaced by some other experience. If you look closely, you will discover that the new experience brought some form of misery. It was simply Misery coming to find his love and reunite with her.

> *The secret to solidifying an intimate relationship with Happiness is to wholeheartedly embrace and welcome our past and present sorrows and heart-hurts, our miseries, into our lives.*

When we choose to welcome both Happiness and Misery as equal partners in the dance of life, they can finally live together and allow their love to weave their wisdom and magic into the fabric of our lives.

Emotional Maturity

Proclaimed atheists seem to be in the minority. Most adults, when asked, say that spirituality in some form is an important part of their lives.

High-minded concepts are health food for the over-burdened mind. There is nothing like a good inspirational concept to lift our spirits and help us to get over the rough spots of day-to-day living. Used correctly, aphorisms and truisms can provide just enough lift to get us out of the doldrums of fear and apprehension that sometimes visit us during trying and stressful times.

I remember when I was going through my divorce and was faced with starting a new life from scratch. I would sit on the balcony after another day of new experiences, responsibilities, and insecurities and attempt to assess my future.

My favorite positive thought at that time was: "Maybe the big earthquake will happen under me and I won't have to do all this." Okay, so I admit that black humor is a part of my Irish heritage but from where I was sitting that was a positive thought.

Like Tarzan swinging through the jungle from vine to vine, concepts held lightly and surrendered easily can bring momentum and fluidity to our obsessive minds and numbed-out hearts.

When concepts are cemented together and used as a protective shield to inform the world that we have arrived at a plane of static perfection and spiritual evolution, that is just plain boring, wrong, and a serious evasion of the facts.

True love and true faith come out of strength, self-reliance, and self-responsibility. For real love and real genuine faith to exist, emotional maturity is a necessary basis.

The ability to love is a direct outcome of emotional maturity and growth. If you want to attain spiritual growth, you have to have emotional maturity.

The intellect responds easily and effortlessly to uplifting thoughts. Spirituality and intellect go hand in hand, a well-matched couple.

What about our pesky, uncontrollable emotions? Where do they fit in? Like the fake arrow that Steve Martin used to wear on his head, we tend to bypass the messy parts of ourselves that are childish, spoiled, resentful, sad, fearful, and confused in favor of building a facade of invincibility that keeps us walled off and protected from our fears of the future and perceived failures of our past.

The only way to keep this protective pretense in place is through rigidity of thought. We try to convince ourselves that through diligent, high-minded thinking we can do this and that we have 'arrived' somewhere.

We were bad and now we are good. We were confused and now we are clear. We were weak and now we are strong. We were hateful and now we are loving. On and on the comparisons go.

We do not grow absolutely or chronologically. Instead, we grow unevenly. We grow partially. We are relative. We are mature in one realm, childish in another.

Our past, our present, and our future mingle and pull us backward, push us forward, or isolate us in the present.

We are made up of layers and with each passage from one stage of our growth to another, we must shed our protective structure. Our emotions leave us exposed and vulnerable but also create the opportunity to cleanse, renew, and gain flexibility once again.

Though we become rubbery and weak-kneed from a bout of emotional meltdown, listening to and accepting our emotional intelligence allows us to shed our old skin and stretch and flex in ways we have never known before.

When we give up comfort spirituality and include our emotions, we can stand with one hand extended into the Universe and one hand extended into the world. We allow ourselves to be a conduit for passing energy.

The true goal of personal growth is to become current with ourselves. Then we can become a conduit of creative energy in the world.

Our intellect joins hands with our emotions and, under the umbrella of the Universal Soul or Spirit, we wake up to present time. Our flexibility increases and allows us the grace of moment-to-moment fluidity and the trust and inner security to let go of our rigid hold on life and ourselves.

When the floodgates of our mind and heart are opened, we become adaptable, versatile, creative, and exquisitely responsive to all aspects of ourselves.

We stand firmly in the present, accepting our immature emotions home. We begin to parent them as they evolve into an increased capacity in us to treat others and ourselves generously, compassionately and with humility because we begin to mature enough to laugh fully and heartily—at ourselves.

Complete Honesty

Is it possible to be honest with another without either violating their boundaries or giving up the right to our own thoughts and feelings?

It is somewhat complicated to answer this question because of the many words that have become synonymous with honesty.

The dictionary defines honesty as: Integrity, uprightness, fairness, justice, equity, trustworthiness, fidelity, faithfulness, honor, freedom from fraud, observance of one's word, genuineness, thoroughness, faithfulness, honor, chastity, virtue, fidelity, morality, sincerity, candor, frankness, ingenuousness, truth, openness, unreserved, plain dealing.

Whew, we have just covered vast moral territory. Let's see how many words it takes to define lying.

Lie: Falsehood, malicious or deliberate falsification, fib, delusion, illusion, fleeting show, falsify, equivocate, romance.

Romance? What is that doing in there? That reminds me of the line in the play *Into the Woods* when the Prince seduces the Baker's wife and when she is upset that he is leaving her, he says it's because: "I'm charming, not sincere". A woman in the back of the audience spontaneously yelled: "Hey, I know that guy."

How can we be honest with others without violating them or giving up our right to our own thoughts and feelings? First, we must be clear about our understanding of honesty and with a definition so loaded with heavy-hitter words, there is a lot of room for misinterpretation.

Let's look at some of the common ways honesty can be mishandled.

For example, in the quest to be honest, we can fall prey to the **Content Honesty Syndrome**. People who came from a background where they were forced to confess all their thoughts, words, and deeds often adopt this habit.

Deprived of psychic privacy and being creative, as all children start out, they split away from their feelings. Why? Because you cannot disclose something you don't know. This is a pretty clever strategy since you get to keep your feelings private and safe. The downside, however, is that unacknowledged feelings become inaccessible to their owner also.

A content honesty communicator tells every minute detail of everything that happens, minus the feelings. The question: "What did you do today?" elicits an answer starting with: "Well, I woke up at 6:45 AM or was it 7:00 AM? I think it was closer to 7:00 AM because I remember glancing over at the clock…" until the listener's eyes glaze over.

The unconscious intent is to be both honest and emotionally safe by giving factual information in great detail and at the same time making sure to disclose nothing of a unique and personal nature.

The next common pitfall is to determine that honesty means total openness, candor, and unreserved disclosure. We could call this **My Life Is An Open Book Syndrome**. This person gifts everyone within hearing distance with access to all her secrets.

She believes that by uncensored sharing of guilts, resentments, fears, sorrows, and apprehensions, she is establishing that she is an honest person. The Open Book Syndrome quickly leads to inappropriate emotional sharing that runs rampant until the listener is overwhelmed and squirming uncomfortably.

The unconscious intent is to be so honest that instant intimacy will be established. "I've told you everything and now we are connected so you won't hurt me. You will understand me."

Though this seems like a different strategy than content honesty, it is used for the same unconscious intent. At best, the communicator can be both honest and emotionally safe. Emotional and mental safety is of primary importance in both examples.

Since feeling both mentally and emotionally safe with another is of major importance to most of us, perhaps we need to alter our original question.

Maybe a better question is: How can we use honesty to be more genuine, honorable, and kind with others? Yes, kind. And let's add caring and consideration while we are at it.

Kindness, caring, and consideration didn't show up in the original definition unless we include them as a part of fairness, equity, and trustworthiness.

When kindness, caring, and consideration are entered as crucial additions to successful interactions with others, the **I Pride Myself On My Honesty So Let Me Level With You** kind of communications become less than desirable.

This is the person who announces that he hopes he can be honest and then goes on to blast holes through others indiscriminately, fueled with unbridled judgments, anger, and resentment.

The recipient of this barrage of candor is invalidated, humiliated, immobilized, and left with no defense. Reduced to rubble.

Then there is the **Righteous Master or Mistress of the Universe Syndrome**. "I know everything so just relax and do it my way."

The trouble with righteousness is that there must be someone who ends up wrong and in a one-down position. I doubt this stance does much toward fostering understanding and inclusion.

I have highlighted four ways to over-exaggerate or misinterpret what honesty really means. We all do them or have done them at some time in our lives.

Here is a quick review. **Content Honesty syndrome. My Life is an Open Book Syndrome. I Pride Myself On My Honesty Syndrome. Master or Mistress of the Universe Syndrome.**

Honesty is a big topic. It might prove productive to take some time to explore your relationship with honesty.

In order to do that, here is a basic rule: If you think the truth will hurt someone, you probably are not down to the real truth yet.

Here are some questions that might be helpful to consider when you are deciding to enter into a truthful conversation about something that is difficult to talk about.

1. Will your honesty create short-term discomfort yet add the real possibility of long-term gains for you both?

2. Are you avoiding telling the truth because you want to stay comfortable, yet when you look closely, you really know that your short-term comfort will ultimately cost you long-term pain or disappointment?

It takes discernment to be willing to pay the price of enduring short-term pain to create long-term gains versus opting for short term comfort that creates long-term pain. These are the main choice options we have when deciding to risk being honest.

3. Are we willing to endure short-term pain and emotional vulnerability for long-term gain or will we opt for short-term comfort and end up with long-term expensive consequences?

Ultimately the truth does set us free but we must be willing to pay the up-front price of vulnerability that true disclosure brings.

It takes courage to speak your truth and it takes discernment to be kind to yourself and others while doing it.

Finding your voice and using it with kindness, care, and consideration creates an opportunity to build a full partnership between your personal power, your intuition, and your core values.

This working partnership allows you to become a discerning, rather than reckless, decision-maker.

Facing Loss and Fears with Grace

When tragedy strikes words are woefully inadequate as we try to wrap ourselves around changes that are too big and far-reaching to assimilate.

When life unexpectedly takes a left turn we find ourselves thrown headfirst into unfamiliar territory. The difficulty is that parts of your life stay the same. You are expected to function as you used to, converse with friends and acquaintances in the old, familiar way, and hold up your end of the bargains you made from the life that is no longer.

Loss and grief are from the same family though they have very different personalities. Loss is an extravert. She enters into our lives boisterously and insistently makes her presence known. Grief is an introvert. You can feel her presence but she takes much longer to speak and never shows her full face all at once.

❧ *When both Loss and Grief enter into our lives, we are unable to walk forward because our feet are each going in different directions.*

One foot is grounded in all the rituals, actions, beliefs, values, and understandings of the life you were building and maintaining while the other foot is groping in the dark for some place to stand.

Loss has many faces. The obvious ones are loss of a loved one, loss of health, or loss of a long-term relationship, a career, or valued possessions.

Cherished hopes, dreams, and plans are the stuff that entertains the mind as we move forward through our daily lives.

When big changes visit, all bets are off. We are thrown into vertigo and must ride the rapids with whatever skills we can muster.

To my mind, the real difficulty comes after the initial storm has passed. After the demolition crew has done its job on the front end, the clean-up is all left up to you.

It is precisely at this time that the full impact of the loss begins to surface. This is when true grieving begins.

There are no words that can comfort because this is not a time of comfort or contentment. Something has been replaced with nothing. A deep hole has been ripped into the fabric of your life. It cannot be repaired, replaced, ignored, or sugarcoated. There is no do-over.

There is no rewinding the tape back to yesterday and most often there is too little impetus available to move forward just yet.

You find yourself standing in present time with no past illusions or future delusions to pad your raw nerve endings. The only truth is that this is a true heart hurt. Your heart has been broken open and your life will never be the same.

At times like these, it can be strangely sedative to know the extent of your own powerlessness. The one power that cannot be stripped from you is the power to do nothing.

It takes a different kind of courage to do nothing until you are led to do something. It is the kind of courage that is required of a woman giving birth.

The first stages of labor are taken up with an internal pep talk where you continue to tell yourself that you can do this, the pain is manageable, it will turn out all right, and there is nothing to worry about.

During the next stage, the pain increases and you are intensely in it and then it passes and you have a moment of relief. As it starts to get intense you counteract the building fear with all the techniques and positive thoughts you can bring to mind because you are still under the delusion that you can use your willpower to maintain control over this situation.

Then comes the moment when you are swept over the cliff. Your body takes over and your ego fades into the background, a helpless participant in an awesome force and power that ushers a new life into form.

Life tragedies are the birth mother of compassion. When your heart is broken open it sends out a song that is the invitation to allow grace to take up residence as a full participant in your new life.

Grace brings her comfort tools: empathy, compassion, and loving kindness that pad the walls of the gaping hole that soon will entertain new vision. When a new vision for your life begins to form everything changes, including the air around you.

Visualization, that seeing of something that is not actually before us, that has not materialized, is an essential and sacred ingredient of new beginnings.

Infant ideas are the harbinger of spring. Though not fully formed, these new ideas let you know that grace has begun the serious task of weaving new dreams that will birth out of the rubble of your devastating loss.

There is no need to hurry the process. There is nothing to do, fix or figure out with yourself—or your life—when grace becomes your life partner. She will fill the empty spaces and shine a light on your next steps when it is time.

You can step into this partnership by asking your intuition, your inner guidance, what is right action for you at this moment.

When you have surrendered into the void, accepting that doing nothing is a holding place until you are shown what to do, you start the process of becoming more intimately attuned to your essence, your core self.

Grace takes your hand and plants your feet firmly facing forward on a wide and solid inner path that unfolds exactly as it should from this moment on.

Fare Thee Well

Farewell is an out-of-fashion way to say goodbye.

The original version, 'fare thee well', expresses a parting wish for someone's welfare. The term welfare is now clothed in negative garb and has lost its connection to its original meaning status which was well-doing or well-being; prosperity. The word 'well' has survived unscathed but when married to 'fare' it sinks down into disparaging free-lunch, user and taker connotations.

Well carries great positive energy in its definition. In good health, fortunate, comfortable, satisfactory, agreeably, favorably, skillfully, intimately, soundly are just some of its definitions.

When well is joined with meaning it births good intentions. When married to 'spoken' it blossoms into cultured speech; being favorably commented on and speaking easily, fluently and graciously.

Since the word well has strong roots, I want to join it once again to fare and elevate welfare to its original prosperous status. So here we go.

When our outlooks on life, our attitudes, are positive and uplifted, we could call them welfare emotions. We feel healthy, fortunate, comfortable, skillful, satisfied, and agreeable. Our feet are firmly planted on the sunny side of the street.

When fortune trips, as it sometimes does, our attitudes and emotions are in jeopardy of sinking down into the quicksand of what is commonly called 'negativity'.

He/she is negative. Don't think negatively. Stop being negative. I hate being around them because they are so negative. That's too negative. Talk about a go-nowhere word.

Most of us are smart enough to know that when we visit our negativity on others, they don't like it. Being negative is the interpersonal kiss of death.

If you ever want more breathing room and a cleared social calendar, start gifting your friends with large doses of your everyday disappointments and frustrations. Before you know it, you will have endless hours of uninterrupted alone time.

Given that negativity is the Midas touch in reverse, why is so much of the information we passively ingest from friends, television, and newspapers predominately negative?

Perhaps we put up with so much external negativity because we are filled with our own negative feelings that we won't address or own.

Maybe we are deeply embarrassed, ashamed, and afraid of opening the internal floodgates that will only bring condemnation or rejection and leave us branded with a label of being negative and therefore problematic, unlovable, or unacceptable.

If we discard using the term negative to define others or ourselves, we can start the process of assessing what attitudes and emotions need a facelift, need to be retired, or need to be acted upon.

Negative emotions, under deeper scrutiny, are simply emergency emotions. The alarm bell goes off, the internal siren sings, the emergency room lights up and, looked at this way, these emotions are our first line of survival mechanisms kicking in to protect and serve us.

Emergency emotions alert us to dangerous internal and external circumstances. When our warning systems are respected and listened to, a friendship with our disowned and disenfranchised emotions can begin.

The benefit of dropping the habit of shutting ourselves off from hearing from the bad, negative, awful, depressed, pick-your-favorite-judgment word part of ourselves; is newfound, clear guidance and direction that is perfectly attuned to our unique life situations.

Being intuitive doesn't mean having supernatural powers that allow us to know our futures. True intuitive power comes from a deep well-spring that transcends good, bad, right, wrong, positive, and negative in favor of a broadened perspective that leaves the comfort-home of labeling and judging for the wide-open exploration and discovery of the unknown in us.

When we court inner prosperity, we are led a step at a time by the light of grace into making new choices that create a real sense of self-trust.

A Leap of Faith

Most of us have faced and lived through life challenges that seemed insurmountable at the time. With hindsight, the remembering of those trying times usually includes the knowledge that we somehow summoned the resources and fortitude to survive the situation.

Kissed by grace, circled in the arms of the angels, supported by the love, caring and concern of friends and family, and opening to new life directions all come together in those tumultuous moments to energetically carry us through and into our future ground.

We start again. We reawaken. We shakily take a step and then another. It becomes a sweet relief at those times that life is always in a state of change. Autumn into winter, winter into spring, spring into summer, summer into fall. Significant life changes, like a stormy and churning ocean, carry us to higher ground and deposit us on unfamiliar shores.

But what of those times when life recedes like low tide? Nothing seems to require much of our attention. We are merely foot soldiers in the march of time. Life yields no surprises, no intrigues.

These are the times that show us our true character and can give us precious opportunities to fine-tune our dispositions instead of our circumstances.

Beneath the surface of our daily life, in the personal history of many of us, there runs a continuous controversy between an Ego that affirms our worth and an Ego that denies it.

Standing up to life's challenges is one test of character. Another, not so obvious, character builder is how we choose to weather the mundane, the ordinary, the uneventful seasons. When the sun has ceased to shine upon us, the creatures of the dark feel free to call.

Old grief, worries, and insecurities vie for guest privileges in the corners of our mind.

A cloak of negativity begins to wrap its arms around us unless we are vigilant and protective of our responsibility and right to choose what thoughts and feelings we entertain during the off-times when we are less engaged and intentional.

Imagine that you are wearing a dark, heavy black cloak woven tightly from the threads of old negative experiences that meld together to form a layer of discontent that threatens to cover you from head to toe.

This dark hooded cloak is fashioned from free-floating fears and all the negative emotions, thoughts, and sensations you experience in your life.

See yourself venturing out into the world with the hood of this cloak pulled right over your head, hiding your face and concealing your true character, your deepest intentions, your highest and best qualities, and a soul full of richness.

Really feel the heaviness of this cloak and how it soaks up the negativity presented by the sellers of fear and apprehension in the marketplace.

Now become aware that this negative cloak can be gradually lifted up and away from your body by you simply choosing to remove it.

Feel it floating away and taking with it all the current negativity that surrounds you. Really feel this cloak loosening and lifting away from you as you breathe in and than let out a sigh of relief.

Imagine the cloak slowly vanishing until it simply fades and disappears from view. Once it is completely gone, you are free to clothe yourself in a new cloak of your choice.

Create a new wardrobe tailored to your unique wishes and desires of the moment. Create a cloak of love, joy, beauty, protection, and safety, or any other quality you choose.

Now choose the cloak you wish to wear right now. Vividly imagine yourself wearing the new cloak you have chosen, this cloak of light and positive energy. See its color and feel its strength and quality all around you.

Realize this new cloak is a symbol of your leap of faith into the moment-to-moment preciousness of life. Know that you have the power and the privilege to clothe yourself in the garment of your true desires.

This garment of your choice will ready you to step into the new life decisions that will assist and allow you to continue on your journey of learning to express the sacredness of your soul.

Loving Well

Before we reach the threshold of the door marked Interdependence, we must first grow conscious of our deep-seated desire to collapse into another with chaotic abandon.

"That's not me," I can hear you saying. "I am probably too independent. I have always been the one to take care of both myself and others. I'm trying to learn how to depend more on others so I'm not always the one in charge."

Let's look a little deeper. When we hold on to a definition of ourselves as fiercely independent, all that really means is that we conveniently gloss over all the times in our lives when we are dependent.

We minimize or erase the contributions others make to who we are, or we operate out of a 'keeping score' mentality to make sure that we are never caught owing anyone anything.

We maintain our strong and always-in-control image at the high price of being emotionally isolated, alone, and unsupported.

Why would anyone choose that? Because it is less terrifying than acknowledging that deep down we each have a desire to collapse and surrender into the strong and capable arms of another.

Those of us who have defined ourselves as independent will not own our dependence needs because of a fear of feeling weak and out of control.

Dependent translates as vulnerable and open to harm for the army of independents striving to keep their one-man/woman show going as scheduled.

Conversely, those of us who define ourselves as dependent simply minimize our own contributions and strengths and keep all the times that we operate independently and the ways that we are in complete control a secret from ourselves and others.

We appear more pliable, open, vulnerable, and in need than we really are. Instead of standing firmly in our own strengths and accomplishments, we hide them in favor of desperately trying to surrender and abandon ourselves into the strong and capable arms of another.

Before we reach the threshold of the door marked interdependence we must grow solid boundaries around our deepest desire to collapse into another with chaotic abandon.

When we throw all of our needs, desires, wants, gifts, talents and abundant caring at another and call it loving them, we only burden and overwhelm them with parts of ourselves they cannot use.

When we have given our all we have succeeded only in abandoning ourselves. Instead of fulfilling another, we have merely reduced ourselves to nothing.

When two people both give themselves up in order to come close to each other, there is no firm ground beneath them. There is too much pleasing, understanding, and surrendering.

Too much yes and not enough no. Too much dependence and not enough independence. The relationship is doomed to a free-fall into helplessness and stagnant disappointment, all in the name of love.

When two people maintain their independent stance and refuse to address or acknowledge their insecurities to each other, distance reigns supreme.

Task focus rules. What we do is more important than who we are. The relationship is maintained by superficial conversations, pat phrases and stagnant, dull, lifeless and 'deadening to the emotions' time together.

Just underneath the surface lives a hyper-vigilance on the part of the partner who feels most insecure. Heartache, loneliness and unfulfilled longings are the true children birthed from 'nothing personal, we are both so strong and complete in ourselves' unions.

⌒ *Before we reach the threshold of the door marked interdependence, we must first grow conscious of our deep-seated desire to collapse into another with chaotic abandon.*

Next, we must grow solid boundaries around this desire and take ownership of it as our own wellspring of unfulfilled longings.

When acknowledged, accepted, and owned we are better able to be both dependent and independent, say yes and no, surrender and stand firm, open and close and fashion a life that is big enough for us to develop, expand, and grow.

When we are willing to accept our own strengths and insecurities, our unfulfilled longings and desires, our gifts and challenges; we can use them as a road map to create a fulfilling life.

We can finally give up living in the safe wading pool of consistent image management in favor of entering the ocean of curiosity where the tides and currents change so rapidly, there is no time for posturing.

When we are ready to live an interdependent life, new questions beg to be asked of our relationships.

1. *Are you challenged, engaged, and intrigued?*

2. *Are you curious about each other?*

3. *Do you revel in each other's strengths and talents?*

4. *Do you explore and marvel at the uniqueness and specialness of what you accomplish together?*

5. *Are you interested and open to learning something new about each other?*

6. *Are you diligent about keeping mental and emotional safety and security vitally alive between you?*

7. *Are you respectful of each other's privacy?*

8. *Do you trust one another with your deepest confidences? Do you listen with a light, accepting ear?*

9. *Do you really see each other?*

10. *Are you considerate, generous, tender, protective, and caring with each other?*

11. *Are you fashioning a life that is big enough for each of you to develop, expand, and grow?*

12. *Are you willing to wrestle with and take responsibility for your own insecurities rather than taking your discomfort with yourself out on your partner?*

The questions that could be asked are endless when we intend to create a life with the seriousness, intent, and passion given to a great adventure.

Instant Intimacy

In our fast-paced society, we have come to expect that everything, including intimacy, can be created instantly. As a result, it can be confusing to determine what level of openness about our personal lives is appropriate to the establishment and continued health of our inter-personal relationships.

With the advent of the internet, e-mail connections are easily made, copious amounts of information is available, and sometimes a new acquaintance can appear to be a relationship-match based solely on one source of information.

Intuition is called our sixth sense because it actually is the ability to synthesize information from our five senses to establish a deeper information stream.

When we meet another face to face our eyes take them in, we hear the unspoken deeper messages, we sense their energy, and can smell and taste the essence of who they really are.

Underneath the surface banter that we all use to begin the process of connection or rejection, a tremendous amount of information is readily available if we allow ourselves to attune to it.

I often get calls from women who have entered into a relationship and become intimately involved based solely on the fact that they have corresponded back and forth through e-mail and phone calls, each time becoming more and more open without having any information about the other person from their other senses.

Now, I only hear about the disasters, therefore my point of view is a bit skewed. Even so, I think it is worthwhile to remember that what we communicate to others about ourselves and what they tell us is only a small portion of what is true or relevant.

Being open and self-revealing is a crucial ingredient in the process of building trust with another. No openness, no trust. Too much openness too soon violates self-trust.

Runaway openness can leave you unsafe and vulnerable to manipulation. It invites others into your inner life before they have been qualified as respectable or honorable enough to be let in.

Openness is a skill that is crucial and a deciding factor in our success or failure in relationships. I want to give you a model that you can use to decide what is appropriate sharing for you.

Our awareness of ourselves can be divided into two levels. The first level is what we are aware of about ourselves and can share quite easily with little or no discomfort. For example, our name, what we do for a living, where we live, and our opinion about the weather.

What sits below this level is more sensitive information. We could call this information 'what I am aware of about myself that makes me more exposed and vulnerable to you as a result of sharing this, therefore, I will be somewhat uncomfortable.'

This is the level that is best managed by your intuitive knowledge about yourself and your intuitive sensing of another. There is a question that needs to be answered before you share sensitive information about yourself.

The question is: Am I willing to take full responsibility and ownership of these thoughts and feelings before I share them with another?

When this question is considered before sharing intimate information about yourself, your history, your wants, needs, desires, dreams, heart-hurts, failures, successes, fears or apprehensions, then you have a green light to share whatever you deem appropriate.

When we are willing to take full responsibility for our openness, we can use our sharing to establish meaningful, substantial, authentic relationships with others.

This under the surface level is a two-edged sword. Our willingness to disclose our private selves is a supreme gift that creates the possibility of birthing timeless friendships and the sharing of life's intimate treasures.

Sharing from this intimate storehouse also creates the experience of being out of control. Once we publish information, it is in the hands of the gods.

This threatens our illusion that we can control how others see us. Openness cracks our well-put together facades and threatens our image management that makes us appear that all is well and under control.

So why would anyone want to take the openness risk? In order to grow we must learn to let go. When we risk exposing our deeper thoughts and feelings, it makes room for new awareness to surface.

In our culture, we commonly have two types of problems with our feelings. We are either unaware of our emotions or our feelings sometimes surge through us with such force that reason becomes impotent.

We are either blind to our emotions or blinded by them. To the extent our emotions are stifled, we lead dwarfed and stunted lives. Our emotions are important to the quality of our lives because they help define what is most important to us. When deciding how open you are willing to be, use this structure.

1. First, what thoughts and feelings are you presently aware of right now and willing to share? Express that. Listen and receive the other person's response.

2. Ask yourself what you are aware of and a bit uncomfortable about sharing. Decide whether you are willing to risk short-term discomfort to share this or not. A yes means a vote of confidence that you are willing to trust yourself and this other person more. A no means that you have reached your trust boundaries and are unwilling to venture forward either because you don't trust yourself or you don't trust them. All this is good information.

Rather than dredging up deep, dark secrets and blurting them out before you are ready, you begin to learn the skill of information management by being respectful and patient with yourself about what you are willing to reveal.

Take calculated risks. Test the water. See whether you can trust the vulnerable areas of your life to another.

The benefits of stretching our willingness to take responsibility to share on a deeper level is increased access to our own emotional richness and the opportunity to be known more fully by those significant others in our lives.

Have You Lost The Magic?

When we have lost our feeling connection with ourselves, our loves, our friendships or our familial relationships, what is the underlying cause?

Yes, there are probably many surface reasons. We are disappointed, fatigued, bored or confused. Maybe there is too much anger, rudeness, sarcasm or criticism coming from us or to us.

Perhaps we are feeling weakened, submissive or have become disinterested or too passive. Life might be delivering up too much craziness, confusion or difficult challenges.

When we have a breakdown in our relationship with others, or ourselves, it often comes down to the fact that we have lost touch with our imaginative perceptions.

We have lost the magic. We become hopelessly enmeshed in psychological labeling. Our heart closes its door and our intellect is left running the whole show by categorizing and name-calling.

Everything and everyone is labeled, as though naming is the same as experiencing. Our significant interactions are reduced down to a dead transference of data.

We overload each other with meaningless trivia and judgments that are unusable for any creative purpose.

> *When our heart participates, it sees receptively.*
> *We seek out friends and loves so that we can see*
> *and be seen through imaginative perception. By*
> *being imaginatively perceived, we are blessed.*

The intellect questions, probes, and looks for the once and for all answer to the problem. Intellect wants the truth, the whole truth and nothing but the truth.

The heart responds in a softer way. It delights in nuances. It works in tandem with imagination. The heart and imagination walk hand in hand on the softer, slower, sunnier side of the street.

Heart and imagination care less about what a person is and more about how they are. Heart smarts have nothing to do with figuring out, categorizing, fixing, rearranging, influencing or making something happen.

The heart wonders instead about the preferences, dreams, tastes, longings and unique ways of this person.

Here is the dilemma.

How can we perceive others through our heart's affections when we are shut down to our own preferences, tastes, longings, wishes, hopes and dreams?

If we continuously probe, push, interrogate, invalidate and second-guess ourselves, how can we ever hope to be truly receptive to another?

Why would anyone make himself or herself visible to us when it is obvious that we manage ourselves with a heavy hand?

When we are hard-hearted, closed off and uncompromising, the lifestream of small pleasures dries up. We become lost in a desert of sameness and disillusionment with no oasis in sight.

So, how do we turn on our heart valve so that we can be open and receptive once again? Let's go back to square one. Wholeness with self. Holiness.

How whole are you? Where is your tenderness, your patience, your kindness, gentleness and wonder residing?

What is your heart deeply longing for?

When was the last time you gave yourself a break, let yourself off the hook and lightened up on your excessive self-criticism and harsh evaluations?

Imagine yourself turning off your judging and categorizing and turning on your sensing and perceiving.

Forget about making something happen 'out there' for a moment. Instead, turn your attention inward. If you listen closely, you may hear your heart whisper: "Here I am. Right here. Can you, will you listen and hear me?" And as you do, little by little, notice the subtle stirrings within.

Slowly, gently, tenderly and patiently begin the process of letting down, letting go, listening, gently opening to and tenderly receiving the light of love so that the holiness of your heart's affections are rekindled and renewed and the magic can return once again.

The Three-Legged Race

A favorite game that was a staple of large community picnics when I was growing up was the three-legged race.

The way it works is that you pair up with a partner and your left leg is tied to your teammates right leg, or vice-versa. The idea of the game is that you move as fast as you can, in tandem, to the finish line without killing yourself in the process.

I understand now why this was a game that was reserved exclusively for the kids. One reason the adults didn't play I suspect is because many of them were already in a continuous three-legged race in their day-to-day lives and so the fun part had become elusive.

It is important to consider a few things before you pick your partner. If you make the mistake of picking someone with a much longer or shorter, faster or slower stride than you, it is a formula for disaster.

The more dominant and driven person simply drags the other one, kicking and screaming, to the finish line. Not a pretty sight.

Rhythm, timing and tempo play a crucial part in the successful navigation of being tied to another person. Awareness of each other, cooperation, a lighthearted attitude and a one-pointed focus on the bigger goal sets the stage for a decent opportunity to stay the course for the long haul.

The first time you sign up for a race, it is usually without much thought. It looks like everyone is doing it, there is a lot of noise and excitement around the promotion of it and so you figure, why not?

Before you know it, someone picks you, you stand still long enough to be tied together and then you are let loose to experience the elation and devastation of hobbling along, resisting, surrendering, wishing for an escape route, forward movement, good partnering, camaraderie and frustration.

Most often, you experience missing the mark on your unformed but hopeful and unrealistic goal of all fun and gain and no loss or pain.

The three-legged race is an apt metaphor for the relationship woes of many adults. Here is what I often see happening with accomplished, success-oriented women who are seeking a long-term committed relationship.

The traditional marriage picture that they grew up with is too small for who they have become. What do I mean? Picture this. For this example, the left leg will represent responsive, receptive, nurturing, relationship oriented qualities and the right leg assertive, active, task-oriented traits.

Woman meets man. Women offers her left leg, the receptive, responsive, feminine energy side to partner with the man's right leg, the assertive, active, task-oriented masculine energy. So far so good.

Because of the demands of our aggressive society, most women who have made their way in the world have developed a strong masculine side, right leg, on their own.

That strength often hasn't been correctly evaluated because strength in women still gets mixed reviews. The man in this equation has a free-floating feminine leg that is usually not taken seriously for the same reason. Soft and receptive is suspect in the too small definition of manly.

So, the left leg of the woman visibly enters into the partnership. The right leg of the man does the same. They tie themselves together and then the trouble begins.

The woman's strong, unaccounted for and free right leg starts doing what it has been trained to do. Move towards the finish line.

The man's right leg is tied to her left one and he has his feminine side, his left leg that is unacknowledged for it's cooperative strength, being overpowered by her right leg that is invisible in the traditional partnership definition but is still strongly making its presence known.

He can't stabilize because an outside force, her masculine, is competing for dominance with his masculine. His masculine is all tied up in roles and expectations of his duties, rights and responsibilities as the traditional male leader.

Meanwhile, all parties abandon his left leg, the receptive feeling side. His masculine is securely tied to her feminine. His left leg is odd woman out.

It is quite easy to ignore and overlook his feeling nature since it is largely treated as unacceptable and unfamiliar territory anyway.

Her masculine, his masculine and her feminine are too busy in their messy power struggle to make room for his more receptive and unacknowledged feeling nature; therefore, he is only halfway in the game.

Old paradigms of the supportive female and the dominant male deny important realities. Everyone has both masculine energy and feminine energy.

When we put in the time and work to claim and take ownership of both our emotions and intellect, receptive and active, yes and no, dependent and independent, left and right legs, we wouldn't even consider hog-tying ourselves up in a relationship definition that is too small.

Instead, we would be free to possess all of our strengths and use them to create interdependent relationships.

> *When two people standing on both legs decide to partner they are free to and able to commit, cherish, support, cooperate, collaborate, create, inspire and use their combined strengths and earned authenticity to support themselves and each other in a partnership that works.*

Deepening Relationships

One of the worst experiences of being the mother of daughters is when they begin to open themselves to the beginning stages of love and the roller-coaster ride of intense feelings and insecurities begins.

Since I have four daughters who are all adults now, I had four opportunities to fine-tune my responses when our home became Heartbreak Hotel.

With my first two daughters, who were sixteen months apart in age, I simply wanted to track the offending guys down and beat them up for hurting them. This was an overpowering urge that I didn't act on but that didn't make the feeling any less fierce.

The lesson that surfaced was twofold. First, that I couldn't protect my children from heart-hurts and second that most of my reactions stemmed from old insecurities of my own that hadn't properly healed.

By the time my youngest daughter was old enough to date, I had formulated a concept about a phenomenon that seems to appear often in relationships.

I see concepts as a way to frame experience so that instead of being overwhelmed and drowned by too much emotion, I can regain some equilibrium so that I can function more effectively.

The best use of concepts is to see them like the vines that Tarzan used to swiftly make it through the jungle.

A concept is simply something to hold on to in order to get over the rough and confusing spots that periodically surface in life.

The key is to use concepts to increase our flexibility and give us permission to take new actions rather than to avoid participating fully by encasing ourselves in a rigid box of old worn-out concepts and beliefs.

Anyway, whenever the girls were struggling with a confusing relationship I would bring out my "reach/withdraw theory."

It has become a bit of a joke at this point because midway into Lisa, Angie, Jennica or Sara telling me about a relationship upset, as I am taking a breath to respond, they say "I know, Mom, reach/withdraw."

So if I have your curiosity sparked now, at least I can share the concept with you and then you can test it out for yourself to see if it is helpful in creating more clarity.

Here is the premise. We all have insecurities. That is a fact, not a fault. The negative aspect of feeling insecure is when we allow our insecurities to limit and control our ability to respond to life.

Insecurity is defined as uncertain, not sure, risky, not confident, exposed, ill protected. Secure is defined as certain, sure, assured, confidant, fixed, fast, firm, immovable, free from danger, protected, insured.

In the world of feeling, we experience the good and the bad, the happy and the unhappy, pleasure and pain. Contrary to just registering such impressions mentally, emotional experience touches us.

Unhappy experiences exist in every child's life. Pain and disappointment are common occurrences. This creates the early, mostly unconscious, conclusion: "If I don't feel then I won't be unhappy."

In other words, instead of taking the courageous step of living through negative, immature emotions in order to give them room to grow and become healthy, we suppress the childish emotions and therefore dull our capacity for happiness and pleasure while not really avoiding the dreaded unhappiness in the long run.

When we orphan our negative feelings, we end up with a different and much more painful consequence of a wrong solution. We experience the bitter hurt of isolation, of loneliness, and of the gnawing feeling of having passed through life without experiencing its heights and depths and without developing ourselves to be the most and best we can be.

Back to the premise of reach/withdraw.

When our need to hide, ignore, or avoid our emotional vulnerability and insecurity in favor of deceiving ourselves into believing that we are much more integrated and mature then we actually are, we begin to distance from ourselves and others.

A painful game of avoidance of intimacy begins because we are disconnected from our own core and therefore are unable to connect with another. A relationship driven by unclaimed insecurities and fear of loss or pain begins.

One person reaches and the other withdraws. Finally the other person decides to give up and all of a sudden the lights come back on and there is a connection.

The electricity flickers on and off until the confusion and appearing/disappearing act becomes too overwhelming and the relationship ends.

If expressing immature emotions earned you punishment as a child or produced an undesired result such as the loss of affection of certain people or a desired goal became unattainable when you expressed what you really felt, then you might feel justified in keeping your insecurities to yourself.

Actually, it is usually true that venting immature emotions usually yields less than positive results.

The mistake here is in thinking that being aware of what you feel requires that you let go of all control and as a result will be seen and treated as though you are weak and unworthy.

The purpose of exposing your emotions is to develop the courage and humility to allow yourself to be aware of what you really feel and then to express it when it is meaningful.

To be guided by our intuition, it is necessary that our emotions be allowed to become reliable. Unless we are willing to own our insecurities rather than projecting them on others, we will be limited to living with stunted emotional capacities.

When healthy emotions can be harnessed to make our intuition reliable, there is a mutual harmony between our thoughts, feelings, and actions.

As a result, we become free to create relationships based on authenticity and the true security that comes from tending to our emotional growth. By accepting and facing whatever is in us, our ability to love and be loved can grow.

In the last analysis, love is the first and the greatest power and ultimately, it is the only power.

Long-Term Relationships

Long-term means that you have survived the roller-coaster, in-your-face, hearts all aglow stage and now the attention and curiosity level has settled down to a consistent, slow, steady, pilot-light kind of flame.

When the newness wears off, relationships usually shift into comfortable, predictable, okay, sometimes boring but safe routines that foster the experience of security and contentment.

In order to bring renewed interest and enthusiasm into your significant relationship, it may be time to increase your communication about what matters to you. At this point you may be asking: "What does this have to do with intuition?" Hang in here and I will try to explain.

The most important people to us are the first ones we objectify. We put them in a box labeled 'known quantity'. We do that to satisfy our deep need for emotional safety and security.

If I define you in my mind and keep you frozen there, at least I can create the illusion that one thing in my life *is* staying constant.

My selective perception will filter out any changes in you so that I can keep my fantasy of safety intact. My rigid intellectual perceptions will dominate my idea of who you are, leaving no room for intuition, new sensations or curiosity to play any role in our relationship.

My intuitive sensing of you goes to sleep and my intellect freezes my experience of you into a pleasant time warp.

Before any of us can open the channels to access new information, it is necessary to make a decision to wake up our intuition, take the reins away from the intellect and shift over into a willingness to seek out and explore the unknown.

I can hear you now. "My relationship is nice, safe and secure. Maybe it is a bit predictable and boring but, as the saying goes, if it isn't broken, don't fix it."

Wise move with appliances but not so in matters of the heart. A better saying regarding relationship health is 'if you want it to survive, keep it alive.'

The boundary lines tend to get blurred in long-term relationships. We often expect the other person to read our minds and know exactly how to make us happy, even if we don't know what we want ourselves.

In order to create new clarity, I am going to ask you to answer a series of questions. The purpose of each question is to create mental clarity and room for your heart to speak its truth.

You will need some quiet, reflective time and an attitude of curiosity. You will also need to give yourself permission to actually find out and hear what your deeper longings are.

Ready?

1. **First question:** *What do you want in your relationship that you are not getting or not getting enough of?*

2. **Next question:** *What are you getting in your relationship that you do not want?*

3. **Third question:** *This one has two parts. What are you withholding from your relationship and what are you giving instead?*

The last question is a bit tricky. It is addressing the common fact that often we withhold something that is important to give to the relationship because it is a risk for us that may make us feel vulnerable. Therefore we give something else that seems easier instead.

For example: We withhold affection and give witty stories. We withhold disappointment and give 'it didn't really matter' instead, or we withhold information and give superficial 'everything is wonderful' or 'everything is awful' instead.

4. **Last question:** *What are your unspoken commands or demands of your partner?*

    The answer to this one has to do with unrealistic expectations that you may be carrying or holding on to from past relationships. Here is where a curious attitude is very important.

Allow yourself permission to spontaneously access your answers.

You may find that you are expecting your partner to fill in your blanks. You might be unconsciously demanding that they fill you up with whatever you feel you are lacking or were deprived of when you were a child.

You may be unconsciously expecting them to be just like your mother or your father, or never like them. You may be expecting them to pay for someone else's bad behavior from your last relationship.

Delving here is sure to turn up some interesting information. This information can be used to assist you to create the opportunity for increased honesty with your partner.

Our self-knowledge base increases the more we take the time to ask and answer questions about what we want in the significant areas of our lives.

The more we know about ourselves, the more open, receptive and accepting we can be with the people we love.

Remember to take the time to share your new insights with your partner and invite him or her to answer these same questions.

There are many benefits that come from opening the door to increased curiosity, interest, and wonder about your deeper needs and desires.

As your ability to cherish and appreciate the beauty of true self-honesty increases, it wakes up, renews, and energizes your capacity to host increased levels of respect, appreciation, interest, and love for all the significant people and opportunities in your life.

Loving Your Life

Reserve some quiet time for yourself, free from outside distractions. Bring along pen and paper. Real paper, not your laptop or computer because using your individualized handwriting is an easy way to bring your intuitive self to the forefront.

Take some time to allow your mind to rewind back to your past. You are looking for people, situations, and events that are the most significant happenings in your life.

Pivotal points. Magical moments. Take-your-breath-away encounters. Sacred interventions.

You may need to muster up a bit of courage because these experiential diamonds may have initially arrived dressed as a lump of coal. You may be reluctant to revisit that life-stopping disaster that set your bones rattling and shook you alive. Take heart.

You will only need to lightly trace over these events because the real intent of sending you back is to allow you to find and reconnect with specific experiences that you know were meant to be.

What do I mean? Let me explain.

If asked for a running commentary on our moment-to-moment experiences, most of us would respond with mixed reviews. It was okay. Acceptable. Terrible. Awful. Just so-so. I'll give it a seven. It wasn't all that bad. The stuff of life.

In every one's life there have been or will be, if it hasn't happened yet, at least one event that has your name on it.

It is that moment that changes the quality and experience of your life forever.

Here is where I pause to give you time to excavate three major change points from the recesses of your mind. If you only locate one major incident that is okay. Don't unnecessarily labor over this.

1. Write down what happened, who was involved, and how it impacted your life.

Now let's go a step further.

2. Bring your mind into the present tense. Who is presently a part of your life about whom you can genuinely say: "*I wouldn't have missed the experience of you for the world.*"

3. What projects, opportunities, or tasks are you presently involved in that you can honestly say: "I wouldn't have missed the experience of doing this for the world."

> *If you can discover just one person or one task that you whole-heartedly vibrate to, you can then connect yourself to the basic rightness of your life.*

Why? Because every single event and experience that you have had in your life had to happen exactly when, where, and how it did so that you would be in the right place to meet that special person, land that 'I was made for this' job, live in your personal paradise, birth the baby, idea, business, or relationship that infuses your life with love.

When we are willing to admit that life has in fact come and singled us out to engage, invest, decide, choose, stand up, stand out, contribute, and be forever altered by the events that have been delivered to our doorstep, we can no longer say that we are not in the game.

We have been chosen to be a part of the team, even if that was not what we thought was the program we signed up for initially.

When you find yourself impatient with life, numbed by the mundane, and longing for the magic of synergistic life events, remember this: **What you are seeking is also seeking you.**

You are in the right place. It is the right time. Your life is progressing exactly as it should. Relax. Let go.

Position yourself to receive the abundance that is all around you. The best is on its way.

A Return Visit to Your Life Path

Imagine that once again, you are standing firmly on your one-of-a-kind, solid inner life path. Take some time to look around and explore the expressions of nature that surround you at this time. Notice how far the path continues up ahead and also take some time to look behind you to see where you have come from and what you have traveled through.

Now, I want you to set your feet firmly on the path but don't start to move ahead at this time. Focus your attention forward and as you do you will notice that there is a figure that is coming to visit you from your future.

This is your Highest and Best Future Self coming to you once again to start a new phase in your process of transformation.

Notice as much as you can about this figure moving towards you. Once he or she is standing in front of you, reach out and make a connection through your hands and establish eye contact. You will actually begin to feel a current of energy pass between you.

Now, your Highest and Best Future Self will turn to face forward and at this time simply step into and merge who you are today with who you will become. I will give you a moment to do that.

Simply take a step forward, merge, and use your gentle breathing by easily and rhythmically breathing in and out, as you simply notice the places where your energy begins to expand.

And now, once again, set your feet firmly on your path, as your Highest and Best Future Self now begins to separate from you and moves once again down the path and into the future. Take a deep breath and settle yourself once again firmly on your unique path as you stand facing forward.

Turn to your left now and as you do, you will be greeted by your feminine energy. She will appear to you in the form that suits you best and so there is nothing for you to do other than to allow her to connect with you through your hands and to appear to you in the form that is most useful to you at this time.

She is a viable part of you and is here to assist you to become more open and receptive to your expressive, creative, feeling nature. Take a moment to allow her to tell you what she most wants you to know about her at this time.

Now ask her anything that you may want to know from her. Ask her now and listen for her guidance. Allow her to take a position on your left side standing next to you and facing forward. Now turn to your right while still standing firmly on your path.

As you turn to your right, you will notice that your masculine energy is standing facing you. He too will appear to you in the form that is best suited to you so there is nothing for you to do other than to allow him to appear to you and make a solid connection with you through your hands and through eye contact.

Your masculine energy represents your active, accomplishing, and boundary-producing energies that protect you as well as assist you to manifest your contributions in the external world. **He is a part of you and is here to assist you to stand up and take right action through clear thinking and the use of discernment in your decision-making.**

Take a moment to allow him to tell you what he wants you to know about him at this time. Next, ask him anything that you may want to know from him.

Know that both your feminine and masculine energies will be traveling with you from this day on. Your feminine energy will assist you in creating more fullness and richness in your life by encouraging you to become more responsive, open, accepting and receptive and to allow you to attract what your heart desires to you.

Your masculine energy is here to give you the strength and impetus to extend your energy out into the world and also to assist you in creating clear boundaries through right use of both yes and no. Your masculine energy will walk on your right side and your feminine energy will be on your left.

And now turn around and face your past by looking back on your path and as you do you will see two children, a boy and a girl, coming towards you.

The boy represents your exuberant, spontaneous, curious, adventurous, and playful energy. The girl represents your sensitivity, your empathetic abilities, your compassion, your longing for deep connections, and your unfulfilled desires.

As they approach you, take a moment to kneel down by them. Turn your attention first to your little boy. He has something to show you and something that he wants you to have that he has been saving and protecting for you.

So when you are ready, simply hold your two hands out in a gesture of openness and receptivity and allow him to give you this gift.

Take a moment to notice what it is and what aspect of yourself he is returning to you. If you don't know just ask him and he will be delighted to tell you. Thank him for the gift and turn your attention to your little girl.

She has a special secret she wants to tell you. Lean down and allow her to get really close to you so that she can whisper this special secret in your ear. She will be whispering a special longing, a secret desire of yours that she has been holding for you and is so happy to activate it in your life by returning it to you now.

Both of these children are so happy to return home to you today because they will now have a place to be where they can be both protected and listened to so that they can take their rightful place in your life.

Scoop them both up and tuck them into your heart, where they will no longer be over-controlled, underused, ignored, or orphaned.

You are now connected to all of your energies. Your masculine active energy. Your feminine receptive energy. Your exuberant little boy energy and your sensitive/feeling and emotionally connected little girl energy.

All of these energies are coming together now to assist you to actualize your Highest and Best Future Self.

Allow your masculine and feminine energies to merge into you now by taking five rhythmic breaths as you allow all of these energies to take their rightful place in your energy field.

Allow your energetic field to expand to house and take ownership of all of the attributes they are bringing to you today.

Face forward and take a few symbolic steps into your future, assured that your transformational journey is in the process of unfolding from this moment on.

And know that who you are destined to become is already present here and now.

~ APPENDIX

The following are some examples from participants in the Unleash The Power of Your Intuition Seminars. It is very important that you give yourself full permission to choose your own words to express your unique, one-of-a-kind I Am and I Am Letting Go statements. These are here to stimulate and spark permission to use your own creativity.

I Am And I Am Letting go Statements

I Am Accepting As Fact That I Am Living In A State Of Grace.

I Am Letting Go Of Justifying My Happiness.

I Am Loving And Appreciating My Life.

I Am Letting Go Of Hiding My Wisdom.

I Am Loved And At Peace.

I Am Letting Go Of Being Victimized.

I Am Embracing And Owning My Essence.

I Am Letting Go Of Restraining My Unique Self-expression And Participation.

I Am Gently Cherished And Safe.

I Am Letting Go Of Worrying How Others See Me.

I Am Joyfully And Gratefully Receiving My Gifts From The Universe.

I Am Letting Go Of Feeling Guilty For Being Cherished.

I Am Entering An Ocean Of Curiosity Where The Tides And Currents Change So Rapidly There Is No Time For Posturing.

I Am Letting Go Of Having To Make It Happen.

I Am Strong And Nurturing To Myself As Well As Others.

I Am Letting Go Of Keeping Things, Situations, And People In My Life That No Longer Have Any Significance Or Support Me In Any Way.

I Am A Power And A Presence; Guided, Directed And Fully Partnered With My Higher Self.

I Am Letting Go Of Feeling Guilty For Standing Up, Standing Alone Or Walking Away From Experiences I Don't Want.

I Am Easily Taking Elegant Chunks Of Time For Myself.

I Am Letting Go Of "Being" Incomplete By Making Decisions That Take Care Of Me.

I Am Giving Myself Space And Time To Heal.

I Am Letting Go Of My Other Story.

I Am Allowed To Discover My True Self.

I Am Letting Go Of Fear Of Rejection.

I Am Taking Responsibility For Creating My Own Rhythm, Timing, And Tempo.

I Am Letting Go Of Discipline As A Nasty Word

I Am Allowing My Life To Flow Easily And Effortlessly.

I Am Letting Go Of Putting A Lid On My Happiness.

I Am Safe.

I Am Letting Go Of Needing A Continual Stamp Of Approval.

I Am Surrendered To Divine Wisdom

I Am Letting Go Of The Emotional Bondage From My Past.

I Am Being Kind To And Gentle With Myself.

I Am Letting Go Of Dragging My Feet And Avoiding Taking Care Of Myself.

I Am Being There For Me.

I Am Letting Go Of Being Off-Balance.

I Am Energized, Supported, And Handling Daily Life With Grace, Ease And Excellent Timing.

I Am Letting Go Of Investing Time And Energy In Things And Situations That I Can't Affect or Are Out Of My Control.

I Am Growing Quiet.

I Am Letting Go Of Rigidly Analyzing.

I Am Clearly On My Path Bathed In Love.

I Am Letting Go Of Denying My Feelings.

I Am Opening My Heart To Imaginative Perception.

I Am Letting Go Of Non-Productive Anger.

I Am Living In Peace And Serenity.

I Am Letting Go Of My Comfort Zone.

I Am Living A Life Of Abundance.

I Am Letting Go Of Being Stretched Too Thin And Running My Life To The Limit.

I Am Loving, Appreciating, And Acknowledging The Wisdom Of Change.

I Am Letting Go Of Worry, Doubt And Apprehension.

I Am Fully Present And Happy To Be Here.

I Am Letting Go Of Allowing Old Pockets Of Sadness, Anger, And Overwhelming Disappointment To Stifle My Gratitude And Appreciation Of Today.

⌒ ACKNOWLEDGMENTS

This book is a culmination of years of intimate, growth-stimulating interactions with many people who have enhanced my wisdom, my knowledge, and my ability to recognize the sound of the voice of truth. There are so many tender, fulfilling moments that are tucked in my heart. These are cherished essence gifts, from the participants in seminars that I have been privileged to facilitate since the early 1970's. My deepest gratitude goes to all of the men and women who have taken the risk to be open, vulnerable, authentic, and courageous travelers, on the road to real.

I have been blessed with timeless friendships and mentored by many wise and wonderful teachers, who crossed my path at the exact moment that I was ready to glean the most value from their entrance into my life. There are a few I want to mention, who are no longer alive, but whose contribution I carry in my soul.

Thank you, William Penn Patrick, for giving me permission to dream bigger dreams by accepting me when I couldn't accept or approve of myself. Bill Doucette, I am fulfilling my promise to you that I will include both men and women in my ongoing work. Gary Gates, I know you would be pleased at how your encouragement that I stay committed to the development of my intuitive abilities has continued, since that first training I took with you. Ann Dee, I think of you so often, and smile at how diligently you encouraged me to add style and flair to my life, my loves, and myself. I can still hear your full, rich, melodious voice, reading my words back to me, with all the dramatic flair that you put into your shows during your singing career.

John Hanley, Randy Revell, Stewart Emery, John Enright, and George Pransky, you added to my personal development and enhanced my facilitating skills by giving me the opportunity to learn and work with each of you at different developmental stages in my career.

Phillip Bonnell, thank you for teaching me so much about business and also about managing by statistics, a skill that, until I met you, I had no interest in or use for, since my management preference had always been through relationship building. You taught me that a marriage between the head and the heart is the most productive way to create results and I have extended that concept into everything that I presently create. Shepherd Hoodwin, thank you for generously sharing my writings with your clients and for always being there, freely contributing your wide range of interests and expertise, whether technical, literary, or just by making me laugh through your insightful and humorous take on life.

Ginny and Mike Anderson, thank you for being family and keeping me connected to my New York roots. Mary Ann Meier, thank you for keeping the memories alive from where we started back in the San Franciso/Marin County days, and Faye and Bill Phillips, thank you for being a consistent presence and support, initially when I was a young wife, mother, and facilitator, and right up to the present. From all of you, I have learned what timeless friendship means and that being connected and surrounded by people you trust is a lifesaver and a true comfort during the tough times.

Elsa Brizzi, thank you for teaching me that mistakes are simply a pause along the path to finding a better way to make life work. Thank you for your solid, unwavering support and for giving me so many opportunities to say: "Sounds like a great idea to me!" Cate Simpson, thank you for all the magic times, wonderful lunches, and heart-stirring conversations we have shared together.

My heartfelt appreciation to Mary Ann Meier, Elsa Brizzi, Faye Phillips, Barbara Roach, Jane Hilgendorf, Cathy Parks, Alicia Wolff, Susan Chancellor, Kathy Arp, Sheila Ivary Marsh, Diane Forsyth,

Susanne Richardson, Coralee Newman, Caroline Saint-Erne, Carol Reynolds, Christine Fugate, Paulina Brown, Deborah Scott, Kim McEntee, Linda Hughes, Kimberly Hackney-Leiter, and Peter Larsen, and a special thank you to Dr. Maret Kunze for introducing me to so many extraordinary people who chose you for your healing abilities and then, because of your recommendation, have participated with me. I am so pleased and proud that you have chosen to walk with me on this transformational journey through the Unleash the Power of Your Intuition seminars during the past fourteen years. It has been a thrilling adventure filled with so much mental, emotional, and spiritual stimulation. Thank you all for your commitment, your involvement, and your individual contributions to my life. As a result of your presence, I love this arena as much today as I did when it first started.

Catharine Cooper, thank you for encouraging me to write and submit a few articles to Jerry Ledbetter. You opened a new avenue of expression for me that has grown into one of the most enjoyable aspects of my life. Stu Saffer, and the staff of *The Laguna Beach Independent News*, I love the opportunity you have given me to write my weekly column. Stu, I think that you brilliantly continue to serve this community through the publications you have created and sustained. I am proud to be a part of your staff and appreciate being included in such a fine effort. I want to express my gratitude to my readers, the residents of Laguna Beach, who have taken the time to call or write in response to the articles that have spoken to you. It is such a heartwarming gift to be connected to so many wonderful people in my community.

Christine Fugate, your suggestion that we meet for lunch that rainy afternoon here in Laguna, was the catalyst to spark the conception of Beyond Intellect. Your encouragement and sharing was the spark that turned "I should" into "I can." Kimberly Leiter, your unwavering belief that this material needs to get out into the world in a broader way, and your seamless surety that it's a "done deal," allowed me to marry the newly born "I can" to "I will." You ignited this journey and I am deeply appreciative.

Coralee Newman, Walt Sutton, Cathy Parks, Jeff Parks, Dinny Beringer, Bruce Larson, Elsa Brizzi, Faye Phillips, Paul Ruggero, Lisa Velasquez, Sara Velasquez, Jennica Nill, and Kim McEntee, I am so grateful to all of you for taking the time to read the rough draft manuscript and give me your valuable feedback. I think you will see your efforts were not wasted and the book has been enhanced as a result.

To my incredibly talented sister, Pat Magers, thank you for so generously allowing me to share your amazing artistic talents. Your paintings add such a vivid and visual power to the messages in the book.

Laura Beggins, my sister-in-law and friend, thank you for your eagle eye and wholehearted, loving involvement in the final proofing.

Linda Hughes, thank you for trusting my work enough to introduce me to your contemporaries in Walt Sutton's Travelers Group. Walt, I will be forever grateful for your introduction to Jan. Jan King, you have contributed your publishing, writing, and mentoring talents to the task of sculpting a massive amount of material into a credible, stand-up body of work. Plus, you made the journey safe, accomplishable, and extremely enjoyable. Patricia Leigh, thank you for lending your artistic eye and photographic talents to this project. You have changed my harsh self-judgment and discomfort with having pictures taken, into one of the most enjoyable and positive experiences in completing the back cover of this book.

Ibrahem Guirguis, and the staff at The Capri Laguna On The Beach, thank you for taking such good care of us during our stay with you, weekly, over the past three years. The warmth and old Laguna charm that the hotel provides adds so much to the experience of safety and trust and, Ibrahem, your hospitality and graciousness is greatly appreciated.

My greatest opportunities for opening my mind and heart, deepening my capacity to love, softening any rigid locks on how life should be, and strengthening my willingness to fully participate in life, come from the bottomless love that I have for my four daughters: Lisa Monet, Angelique Helene, Jennica Lynn, and Sara Christine. I cherish the opportunity I have had to be your mother and wouldn't have missed it for anything in the world.

Now that you are all adults, you have become invaluable door openers to new experiences and information that is outside of my knowledge base. Thank you for including me in your lives, for your encouragement, and your insightful, astute, and kindly delivered feedback, throughout this process. It is thrilling to be on the receiving end of your brilliant and creative minds, your quick wit and your generous love.

Susan McNeal Velasquez

Spring of 2007

A Special Tribute to William Lee Grover
May 13th, 1926 – May 19th, 2006

With gratitude from all those that loved him and deep
appreciation for the legacy he left behind.

ABOUT THE AUTHOR:

Susan McNeal Velasquez, a Master Facilitator, has been writing and producing personal development seminars since 1972.

Susan has served as the Executive Director of Leadership Dynamics Inc. and was involved in the startup of Lifespring Inc. as a Basic and Advanced Trainer. She was co-creator of Interact Relationship Seminars and the creator of Prime Time Seminars.

Additionally, she spent six years as the Executive Vice President of Verbal Advantage Educational Programs.

She is currently a columnist for *The Laguna Beach Independent News* and presents ongoing seminars on the topic of how to Unleash the Power of Your Intuition. She is a Life Coach for experienced coaches and small business owners who want to increase their ability to trust their intuition.

Her strong business background coupled with her unique and dynamic style makes her one of the most experienced personal development facilitators in Southern California.

She can be contacted at: **www.BeyondIntellect.com**
1278 Glenneyre St. #83
Laguna Beach, CA 92651
Email: **susanvelasquez3@gmail.com**

⌒ ABOUT THE ARTIST:

Pat Magers is a professional artist who currently resides in Atlanta, Georgia. She has an MFA in drawing and painting from Georgia State University, Atlanta, Georgia and a Bachelor of Arts, Summa cum Laude, Olivet College, Olivet, Michigan.

Pat is sought-after as a commissioned portrait painter, is a master landscape and seascape artist, and is proficient with both oil and water-color. She has also done freelance advertising illustration for Alexander/ Pollard Agency. Clients included Delta Airlines, Coca-Cola Company, Random House Publishing, and Scholastic Books.

She has successfully competed in many juried shows and is currently showing in galleries throughout Atlanta.

More of her work can be viewed at: **www.PatMagers.com**

INDEX

A
acceptance, 48–50
anti-intuitive behaviors, 42–44
anxiety, 58
attention, 18-21, 30-32
attitudes, life-changing, 157–158
authentic, being, 16–17
    congruency, 46–47, 67–69

B
best future self, 38–40

C
ceasefire, calling, 82–84
change
    controlling, 76–78
    fear of, 75
choice, 18–19
congruency, 46–47, 67–69
Content Honesty Syndrome,
    164–165
cottage in the woods, 101–103
courage to be happy, 154–156
A Crack in the Cosmic Egg, 57
creativity, opening, 91–94

D
decision-making, 130–132
deepen, 130–132
dependence, 175–178
doors, 121–123
    decision-making, 130–132
    deepen, 130–132
    open to, 135–137

    soften, 123–130
    strengthen, 140–144
    unknown, celebrating, 137–140
    yes vs no, 132–135
Double Dutch approach, 50–52

E
emotional maturity, 160–163
energy audit, 104–107
exercises
    cottage in the woods, 101–103
    I AM, 32–34
    I AM Letting Go, 34–36

F
family life, 71–73, 111–112,
    117–119, 186–189
fear, types of, 16, 57–58
freedom, making a run for, 60–62
friendships, 69
fulfillment, 50–52

G
going to nothing, 98–100
grace and grit, 142–144
gratitude, 157
grief, 167–170
guidelines for using book, 13–14
guilt, 57

Printed in the United States
87919LV00001B/139-300/A